THE ORIGINS OF
The School for Scandal

THE ORIGINS OF
The School for Scandal

"The Slanderers"
"Sir Peter Teazle"

Edited by Bruce Redford

Richard Brinsley Sheridan.

PRINCETON UNIVERSITY LIBRARY
PRINCETON, NEW JERSEY
1986

Published under the sponsorship of
the Friends of Princeton University Library

Printed in the United States of America
by Princeton University Press
at Princeton, New Jersey

CONTENTS

FOR
ROBERT H. TAYLOR
in memoriam

FOREWORD

The Robert H. Taylor Collection came to the Princeton University Library in two stages. Born in Gloucester, Massachusetts in 1908, Mr. Taylor attended the Riverdale (New York) Country School and in 1926 entered Princeton University where he majored in architecture. He lived in Yonkers, New York, until he moved to Princeton in 1960. During the next decade the University Librarian, William S. Dix, persuaded him to consider refurbishing a room contiguous to the Rare Book Department of the Firestone Library and depositing there his growing collection of books, manuscripts, and drawings in English and American literature. It arrived in 1971, still a private collection although integrated with the Library's card catalogue for the benefit of faculty and students. From that year until his death in May 1985 he continued to enlarge what was already a magnificent gathering of more than 5,000 volumes. The obituarist of *The Times* of London called it "one of the most distinguished collections of books and manuscripts of English literature made in this century" and announced prematurely what only the Taylor will could confirm: "Princeton University Library . . . now becomes the final home of such a collection as can never be made again."

Robert Taylor made his first purchase as a schoolboy on a non-existent book budget, a 1794 edition of Samuel Johnson's *Lives of the Poets*. "I pored over it most of the night," he recalled many years later, "reminding myself frequently that this was the way the work had looked to its original readers." As a Princeton undergraduate he was addicted to the novels of Anthony Trollope. Since there was no collected edition available he was "reduced" to buying first editions from the Princeton branch of the Brick Row Bookshop. Thus he began "assembling," without being aware of it, the first of the "Taylor authors." From Trollope he moved to Pope, Sheridan, Byron, and Beerbohm with the help of David A. Randall at Scribner's, Michael Papantonio of the Seven Gables Bookshop, and Dudley Massey of Pickering and Chatto in London. "I felt," he said, "that these authors were representative of their respective periods and could still be collected with some approach to completeness."

Contemplation of the Richard Brinsley Sheridan archive now at Princeton makes the word "complete" seem inadequate. Herman W. Liebert, Librarian Emeritus of the Beinecke Library at Yale University, has described its manuscript treasures in the special Taylor Collection issue of the *Princeton University Library Chronicle* (Winter-Spring 1977). After Mr. Taylor's purchase in 1982 from Bernard Quaritch, Ltd of the collection assembled by Pickering and Chatto—an unrivaled assortment of early printed Sheridan material—we asked Bruce Redford, Professor of English at the University of Chicago, to describe in the *Chronicle* (Spring 1985) what this new acquisition meant. In his article on the archive, he summed it up in one sentence: "Thanks to this purchase, which swells its Sheridan holdings by 690 items, the Taylor Collection must now be considered indispensable to every kind of scholarly enterprise [on the subject]—critical, biographical, and bibliographical."

The next step was inevitable. To celebrate the acquisition, we discussed a facsimile publication of some part of the Sheridan manuscripts. The Council of the Friends of the Princeton University Library—Mr. Taylor had been its chairman for 26 years—was willing to underwrite the project as it had in 1982 when Professor Lawrence Danson introduced another Taylor manuscript to the scholarly world in his fascinating reconstruction called *Max Beerbohm and The Mirror of the Past*. Mr. Taylor asked Professor Redford to transcribe Sheridan's two holograph sketches which preceded, in seminal state, his masterpiece, *The School for Scandal*, produced at Drury Lane in 1777. They began working together in the Taylor Collection in the summer of 1984. But Professor Redford is the specialist on Sheridan and his contemporaries. He can speak for himself in the introduction which follows.

Richard M. Ludwig
Associate University Librarian
for Rare Books and Special Collections

INTRODUCTION

"It is pleasant," declares Dr. Johnson in his *Life of Milton*, "to see great works in their seminal state, pregnant with latent possibilities of excellence; nor could there be any more delightful entertainment than to trace their gradual growth and expansion, and to observe how they are sometimes suddenly advanced by accidental hints, and sometimes slowly improved by steady meditation."[1] The two playlets reproduced here, "The Slanderers" and "Sir Peter Teazle,"[2] preserve in its "seminal state" the finest English comedy of the eighteenth century—a fit successor to *The Way of the World* and precursor of *The Importance of Being Earnest*.

This pair of manuscripts teems with "latent possibilities of excellence." To study them carefully is to enter Sheridan's dramaturgical workshop, to participate in the "growth and expansion" of a masterpiece. Their importance as holograph sketches, moreover, is enhanced by their rarity: apart from the Frampton Court MS, a late draft of *The School for Scandal*, no other foul-papers of comparable significance have survived. The manuscripts of *The Rivals* had vanished by the early nineteenth century, and *St. Patrick's Day*, *The Duenna*, and *The Critic* were lost at sea in the 1930's. Though Thomas Moore included generous excerpts from the two playlets in *Memoirs of the Life of the Right Honourable Richard Brinsley Sheridan* (1825), his transcripts are unreliable: not only does he misread and repunctuate, he also rewrites at will. Most students of the play have accepted Moore's versions uncritically and based their findings upon them. It is only by scrutinizing the originals, however, in all their untidy complexity, that one can begin to formulate sound conclusions about the genesis of the play and the workings of Sheridan's creative imagination.

What is it, in specific terms, that the manuscripts tell us? A reasonably comprehensive response to this question would include at least five points (each one of which will be expanded and illustrated in the pages that follow). First, it is now indisputable that the sketches were not conceived as separate plays but as different facets of the same play. Second, *The School for Scandal* as we know it originated in a scattering of *bons mots*, witty epigrams or turns of phrase around which Sheridan wove his comedy. Third, the playlets exemplify a method of composition that is based on ceaseless reworking and refinement of fairly crude first ideas. Fourth, they testify both to the influence of Restoration models and to a keen awareness of contemporary taste. Finally, the sketches lay bare the problematic yoking of satirical repartee with sentimental melodrama that was Sheridan's single major defect as comic dramatist.

Thomas Moore's oft-repeated claim that "the two plans are entirely distinct" was first called convincingly into question by Cecil Price, who pointed out several connections between them.[3] As Price observes, Maria the ingénue appears in both sketches; furthermore, the stratagems of the two villains (Lady Sneerwell and Young Pliant respectively) take effect by means of the same kind of scandalous insinuations. Nevertheless Price fails to make use of three pieces of evidence that clinch the argument for consanguinity. First, at the beginning of the second "Sir Peter Teazle" copybook occurs the notation, "Crabtree to wear a Muff." "Sir Christopher Crab," "that ridiculous old Knight" and the uncle of "Sir Benjamin Backbite," figures prominently in "The Slanderers." By the time Sheridan came to write "Sir Peter Teazle," he had lost a title and changed from "Crab" to "Crabtree." Second, the name "Babble Bore" appears among the jottings on the last page of the "Slanderers" MS, "Sr Babble bore" on the inside back cover of the second "Sir Peter Teazle" notebook. Like "Lady Baulwell," the name may have been an early idea for a victim of the Scandal Club. Third, a note on the penultimate page of "The Slanderers," "to sin in her own Defence," supplies the germ of Lady Teazle's celebrated *mot*: "So then—you [would] have me sin in my own Defence—and part with my Virtue to Preserve my Reputation" (p. 102). The first hints for the second half of the same paradox appear as "loose her Vertue to preserve her Reputation," a phrase jotted on the final page of "The Slanderers." All these cross-references, however fragmentary, force us to discard Moore's hypothesis for good. No longer will it be possible to speak, in John Loftis's phrase, of "the two distinct components of the play."[4]

Further evidence of close kinship is not far to seek. Comparison of the two manuscripts with each other and with the Frampton Court MS reveals that both playlets were sparked, not by memorable characters or dramatic confrontations, but by half-formed witticisms, insinuating turns of phrase, inchoate epigrams. Some of these notes did not advance beyond the stage of what might be called verbal doodling. The two "Sir Peter Teazle" notebooks yield several examples of such stillborn wit: "Tie up the Knocker of her Tongue" (p. 164); "going to Julia they are to leave their Wives and their consciences at Home" (p. 134); "His common Conversation on the subject would serve to open an Hospital Chappel" (p. 144); "if he was to lose a Hair whenever he tells a lie He'd be bald in four and twenty Hours" (p. 134). Other preliminary ideas, amplified and pointed, do find a permanent home in dialogue. We have already taken note of the two half-lines from "The Slanderers" that unite to form Lady Teazle's famous paradox. Less predictable changes can also be plotted. Four cryptic words, for example—"Charards—my First—is"—grow into Crabtree's opening speech, "I'll back him at a Rebus or a Charade against the best Rhymer in the Kingdom. . . ."

Expansion is one kind of change, fine tuning another. Sheridan excelled at the subtle adjustment of a witticism: the core of a particular *mot* will often be preserved intact, but its setting rearranged for greater cumulative impact. Sir Oliver's criticism of valets who ape their betters starts out: "Servants used to have only the cast vices of their masters—but now they have him [sic] like their Birth Day Cloath with the Gloss on them" (p. 134). This is emended to read: "Master Rowley in my Day Servants were content with the Follies of their Masters when they were worn a little Thread-Bare but now they have their Vices, like their Birth-Day Cloaths with the Gloss on."

In the beginning was the verbal pattern—and words retain their primacy through every surviving stage of the play's development. According to J. R. Jackson, who examined the two sketches twenty-five years ago, Sheridan "was prepared to accept or ignore flaws of plot or character in order to preserve favorite aphorisms intact—in short . . . his eye was upon dialogue rather than action."[5] In fact, one could go so far as to say that plot exists for the sake of aphorism. What was most important in Sheridan's mind was that line *x* be uttered, and uttered with maximum éclat—not that line *x* be in character or that it advance the action. Accordingly, lines tend to be moved about from character to character in keeping with the rhythms of a given scene. One example will stand for many: an exchange in "The Slanderers" between Mrs. Sneerwell and Sir Christopher Crab ("Nay— She has charming Fresh Colour— / Yes when tis fresh put on") is reassigned without qualm to Mrs. Candour and Lady Teazle.

"The Slanderers" and "Sir Peter Teazle" illustrate the first two stages of the creative process: the movement from disconnected jottings to snatches of dialogue, and from dialogue to extended scenes. Progress it is—but progress of a limited kind. Never did such humble beginnings, one is forced to conclude, lead to such a brilliant outcome. In truth, Sheridan's earliest intimations of the play we call *The School for Scandal* prove, to quote Thomas Moore, "as little like what it afterwards turned into as the block is to the statue, or the grub to the butterfly."[6] As the manuscripts testify on virtually every page, Sheridan roughed out his ideas at top speed, then subjected them to painstaking correction. In this respect he resembles no one so much as Alexander Pope, the greatest verbal craftsman of the century. *Mutatis mutandis*, Pope's method was Sheridan's: "to write his first thoughts in his first words, and gradually to amplify, decorate, rectify, and refine them."[7]

The activities of rectification and refinement can be traced in the language, characters, and dramatic pacing of the play. Before analyzing the evolution of the three principals—Sir Peter, Lady Teazle, and Joseph Surface—we should pause to survey those changes in verbal texture which accompanied and reinforced developments in characterization. The two sketches demonstrate Sheridan's flair for pointing an epigram: Lady Sneerwell's "it is absolutely impossible to be witty without being a little ill natur'd" (p. 34) turns into "there's no possibility of being witty—without a little ill nature." The obvious is muted, as when "Miss Shepherd of Ramsgate" changes her name to "Miss Letitia Piper," and "Lady Baulwell" becomes "Lady Dundizzy." We can also observe Sheridan honing and redistributing details, touching up satirical portraits, and converting long speeches into lively stretches of comic stichomythia. All three such activities transform Sir Peter's original speech of reminder and reproach (pp. 74-76) into a playfully antiphonal vignette of pastoral stultification. The relevant passages are too long to quote in full, but the fortunes of a single detail will give an accurate indication of Sheridan's transmogrifying genius. Initially Sir Peter is made to number among his wife's former accomplishments the ability "to play country Dances—on an old Spinet to your—Father while he went to sleep." Perhaps with Sophia and Squire Western in mind, Sheridan then inserted: "to play him to sleep after a Foxchase." The line in the Frampton Court MS reads: "to strum your Father to sleep after a Fox Chase." The same phrase is finally transferred (with the necessary change of pronoun) to Lady Teazle, a move that helps to eliminate the vituperative tone of the original speech.

Sir Peter Teazle begins life as "Old Solomon Teezle," a Plautine *senex*-figure who has "left off Trade" but not fleshly desires. The playlet named after him opens with a soliloquy in which he laments his inability to do without a wife. Ignoring the lessons of bitter experience, "Old Teezle" has recently married for the third time. His new wife, a country girl thirty years younger than he, is rapidly dissipating his fortune. On her unheralded appearance (p. 78), he turns without warning into "Sir Peter," and in the process sloughs off the grossness and the self-pity that marked his opening speech. The contrast between its harsh, unforgiving final lines ("what a Defect it is in our Laws—that a man who has been once branded in the Forehead—should be hang'd for the second Offence") and Sir Peter's rueful confession ("Yet the worst of it is I doubt I love her or I should never bear all this," I.ii) is one measure of the comic sea-change the character undergoes in a matter of three pages.

The *Ur* Lady Teazle plays the role of May to her husband's January. Sly, selfish, and mercenary, she refers to Sir Peter as "the old Curmudgeon" and declares to Young Pliant, the prototype of Joseph Surface: "O Hang him—I have told him plainly that if He continues to be so suspicious I'll leave him entirely and make him allow me a separate Maintenance" (pp. 98-100). This Lady Teazle has married simply to escape from the boredom and straightened circumstances of country life. She does not hesitate to inform her husband that she wishes to become a widow as quickly as possible. When Sir Peter asks her, "if I were to die what would you do," she replies callously, "countermand my new Brocade" (p. 84). To the sorrowful half-question, "Then you never had a Desire to please me or add to my Happiness," she responds brutally, "Seriously I never thought about you—did you imagine that age was catching—and I think you have been overpay'd—for all you could bestow on me" (p. 86). This late eighteenth-century cousin of Wycherley's Margery Pinchwife goes to Young Pliant's ready to be seduced, and is close to giving in when her husband unexpectedly arrives.[8] For all these reasons her contrition at the end of the screen scene is much less credible than in the later versions of the play, when the "glare and coarseness" of the character have been toned down.[9] One change in particular epitomizes the difference between rough sketch and nuanced portrait. The first Lady Teazle declares crassly, "if you have a mind to make me more grateful still make me a widow" (pp. 84-86); her more tactful reincarnation responds with a gentle cough to Sir Peter's "My widow I suppose?" (II.i).

Young Pliant (also called "Plausible") is a fit partner to the original Lady Teazle: a nasty trouble-maker, with crude appetites and ambitions, he has yet to acquire a suave, "sentimental" gloss. His first soliloquy reveals a penchant for maneuvers reminiscent of Fielding's Blifil:

> . . . I think we have taken care to ruin my Brother's character beyond his Power to retrieve it with my unkle should He arrive tomorrow. Frank has not an ill Qu[a]lity in his Nature—yet a Neglect of Forms and of the opinion of the World has hurt him in the Estimation of all his graver Friends—I have profited by his Errors—practiced to gain a Character—which now serves me [as] a mask to lie under. . . .   (p. 98)

Unlike Blifil or Joseph Surface, however, Young Pliant's sexuality lies so close to the surface that it threatens to subvert his plot: "a very difficult Part I have to play here—I must by no means shrink from the Pursuit of Maria—yet have the spright[l]y Attractions of this little Rustic stole into my Heart so that I am led to risk my Interest with Sr Peter—and sacrifice my Policy to my Passion" (p. 156). Thwarted in his designs, he turns viciously on

"Mr. Stanley": "Well let him starve—This will serve for the Opera" (p. 154). Whereas Joseph preserves his finesse even when the game is up ("Moral to the last drop!"), Young Pliant lapses into boorish anger. His transformation from playlet to play is analogous to Lady Teazle's: both are endowed over successive drafts with a complexity of motive and a facility of language that go far toward disguising their cartoon-like origins.

Not only does Sheridan polish his major characters and the dialogue that defines them, he also rethinks the shape of important confrontations. For example, the scene of mutual recrimination in "Sir Peter Teazle," which seems both rhythmically tentative and tonally uninventive, Sheridan divides into two (II.i, III.i). This change has several advantages: it dispels the atmosphere of monotonous inquisition, it embroiders the themes of expense and ingratitude, and it creates the impression of a playful, fundamentally loving *discordia concors*. Similar advantages accrue from refinements in the great screen scene. In the original version Sir Peter hides himself behind the same screen as Lady Teazle. Sheridan realized how improbable the action was, and by redirecting Sir Peter to a closet on the other side of the stage, he devised one of the most comical sequences in the play. Sheridan also improved the ending of the scene by eliminating Sir Peter's challenge to Young Pliant. In place of the summons to a duel, a theatrical cliché with the additional disadvantage of being psychologically improbable, he has Sir Peter cut short one of Joseph's "sentiments" with a quick exit. The superiority of honest deeds over hypocritical words is thereby dramatized with economy and vigor.

The influence of Restoration comedy on *The School for Scandal* has long been a critical commonplace. Not only did Sheridan read and imitate, however, he adapted as well: immediately before starting work on *The School for Scandal*, he remade Vanbrugh's *The Relapse* into *A Trip to Scarborough*. The censorship exercised on Vanbrugh's bawdy text—what the *London Evening Post* called "a judicious pruning of the *licentious* parts"—turned into self-censorship when he began to refine the preliminary sketches for his own play.[10] The analogy is strikingly precise: *The School for Scandal* is to "The Slanderers" and "Sir Peter Teazle" as *A Trip to Scarborough* is to *The Relapse*.

Operating first on his predecessor and then on himself, Sheridan transforms the brazen into the oblique, the crude into the elegant, the amoral into the moral. David Garrick's prologue for the original production of *A Trip to Scarborough* suggests the criteria, at once aesthetic and social, that guided these acts of surgical reconstruction: "Those writers well and wisely use their pens, / Who turn our Wantons into Magdalens. . . ."[11] In fact, Clerimont's "Deceitful wanton" (p. 62) does not reform so much as vanish entirely, while Sir Peter's "Damnable" dwindles into "Horrible" (p. 124), Lady Teazle's "debauchd" into "seduced" (p. 128), and Mrs. Candour's "Bagnio" into "a house of no extraordinary Fame" (p. 36). In what spirit—mercenary or moralistic or both—Sheridan undertook such changes is impossible to determine. But the record of his career as manager of Drury Lane indicates that he would do anything to please (and therefore not to offend) the tastes of his audience: "The drama's laws the drama's patrons give. . . ." His own private inclinations tended toward the direct, the earthly, the unrefined. What the playlets represent, in effect, is the equivalent to familiar letters or conversation: private memoranda of ebullient first impulses that must be carefully disciplined before they appear in public.

As he conflated, amplified, and refined the two playlets, Sheridan strove to fashion a convincing generic hybrid—a cross between punitive and corrective satire, comedy of wit and comedy of sentiment. Of all the major characters, Lady Sneerwell most clearly betrays these mutually exclusive goals. Oscillating between the epigrammatic and the bombastic, she skewers her acquaintance one moment and rants extravagantly the next:

> Maria—have you so little regard for me? would you put me to the Shame of being known to Love a Man who disregards me—had you entrusted me with such a Secret—not a Husbands Power should have forced it from me! but do as you please—go—forget the Affection I have shewn you—forget that I have been as a mother to you whom I found an orphan—go break thro' all ties of gratitude and expose me to the worlds—Derision to avoid one sullen Hour from a moody Lover. (p. 30)

Maria of "The Slanderers," by the same token, has wandered in from sentimental melodrama. Yet even Sheridan, with all his weakness for the histrionic, knew better than to preserve her most egregious examples of moralistic posturing. Thus the refusal to join in "a little harmless Raillery" ("I never can think that Harmless—which hurts the Peace—of Youth—draws tears from Beauty—and gives many a Pang to the Innocent," p. 32) loses much of its original priggishness: "if to raise malicious smiles at the infirmities and misfortunes—of those who have never injured us be the province of wit or Humour Heav'n grant me a double Portion of Dullness" (II.ii). Despite such attempts to preserve a uniformly brilliant verbal texture, however, uncomfortable shifts in tone and patches of stale diction survive to betray the act of miscegenation that produced *The School for Scandal*.

NOTES

[1] *Lives of the English Poets*, ed. George Birkbeck Hill (Oxford: Clarendon Press, 1905), I, 124.

[2] Cecil Price, following R. Crompton Rhodes, refers to the longer playlet as "The Teazles." See *The Dramatic Works of Richard Brinsley Sheridan* (Oxford: Clarendon Press, 1973), I, 291ff. I have adopted the title as it appears on the cover of both notebooks, viz. "Sir Peter Teazle."

[3] Moore, *Memoirs*, p. 165; Price, I, 293.

[4] John Loftis, *Sheridan and the Drama of Georgian England* (Cambridge, Mass.: Harvard Univ. Press, 1977), p. 96.

[5] "The Importance of Witty Dialogue in *The School for Scandal*," MLN, 76 (1961), p. 601.

[6] Moore, p. 162.

[7] *Lives of the Poets*, III, 219.

[8] As Mark S. Auburn observes, "This Lady Teazle evidently knows her own mind. She has planned ahead for this meeting, and now she wants confirmation of his constancy to her, much as in the manner of the Restoration love game." See *Sheridan's Comedies: Their Contexts and Achievements* (Lincoln and London: Univ. of Nebraska Press, 1977), p. 120.

[9] Moore, p. 171.

[10] Quoted in Price, II, 558. For a concise account of Sheridan's changes, see Price, II, 555-56 and Loftis, pp. 79-80.

[11] Price, II, 571.

A NOTE ON THE MANUSCRIPTS

"The Slanderers" is bound before the Frampton Court MS of *The School for Scandal*, which has been interleaved with Thomas Moore's edition of the play. According to a note in the hand of Sheridan's grandson, the sketch "was written in a School boys copy-book. On the outer leaves of which, at the commencement and end, will be found written a number of stray thoughts and scraps of dialogue." The pages have been numbered and bound out of order; the present edition restores the correct sequence, and reproduces the exact size of the original.

"Sir Peter Teazle" occupies two notebooks, each containing 26 leaves. The pages of both are unnumbered. The first notebook is almost entirely filled. The second notebook contains only 15 pages of notes and dialogue, beginning with "Crabtree to wear a Muff" and including the conversation between Joseph Surface and "Mr. Stanley." Only pages with writing on them have been reproduced, each in its actual size.

The manuscripts were written almost entirely in black ink that has faded to various tones of brown. The one exception is the penultimate page of the second "Sir Peter Teazle" notebook, which is written in both red and black. The red ink has faded to a very pale pink, so faint as to be illegible in places.

TEXTUAL NOTE

Without attempting a diplomatic transcript, I have adhered as closely as possible to Sheridan's holograph. At the same time I have also taken certain editorial liberties. The justification for these is twofold: first, the transcript is meant to be legible as well as faithful; and second, the interested reader is free to consult the original at any point, or even to ignore my version of it. Accordingly, I have normalized spacing, indentation, and interlineation. Superscripts have been lowered, and standard abbreviations (e.g. "&" for "and," "ye" for "the") silently expanded. Only substantive deletions and alterations have been recorded.

Certain typographic devices have been used to mark passages in Sheridan's holograph that are difficult to transcribe consistently. They are listed below, together with examples.

~~has~~ is	One line struck through a word indicates that Sheridan chose to delete it, and to replace it with the word immediately following. Where Sheridan first writes one word, then crosses out part of it to make it another word, it is transcribed as de~~parted~~termined.
~~of~~ from	Two lines struck through a word indicate that Sheridan changed it to the word which follows by writing over the original word. Where he has written over some syllables, thereby changing the word, it is transcribed as insu~~rmount~~perable.
//Lady//	Words set off by diagonal slashes are interlinear or marginal additions whose proper location in the text is uncertain. Where they have been deleted by Sheridan, a line is struck through, as //~~Lady~~//
⟨Babble Bore⟩	Angle brackets are placed around words or phrases which appear to be Sheridan's notes to himself, or asides which he may have intended to use in other sections of dialogue.
wait[ing]	The material inside brackets has been inserted by the editor to complete words, or to supply missing words as required by the sense of the passage, or to call attention to peculiarities of spelling, usage, or syntax that may give the reader pause.

THE SLANDERERS

THE SLANDERERS

Lady Sneerwell and Spatter

Lady Sn—	The Paragraphs you say were all inserted —
Spat.	They were ma'am —
Mrs S.	Did you circulate the Report — of Lady Brittle's Intrigue with Captn Boastall —
Spat.—	Madam by this [time] Lady Brittle is the talk of half — the Town — and in a week — will be toasted as a demirep —
Mrs Sneerwell.	What have you done as to the innuendo — of Miss Nicely's Fondness for her own Footman —
Spatter.	Tis in a fine train ma'am — I told it yesterday to my hair-Dresser — he courts a millener's girl in Pall-mall whose mistress has a first Cousin — who ~~has~~ is wait[ing]woman — to Lady Clacket— I think in about fourteen hours — it must reach Lady Clacket — and then you know the Business is done —
Mrs S.—	But is that sufficient — do you think?
Spatter	O Lud Maam — I'll undertake to ruin the Character of the primmest Prude in London with half as much — Ha! ha! did your La'ship never hear — how poor — miss — wortley[?] — lost her Lover and her character — last Summer at Scarborou[gh] — — this was the whole — of it — one Evening at Lady Leringer's the conversation happen'd to turn on — the Difficu[l]ty — of breeding nova Scotia Sheep in England — I have known instances says — says miss Lamb —

Lady Sneerwell & Spatter

Lady Sn — The Paragraphs you say were all inserted —

Spat. — They were ma'am —

Mr S. — Did you circulate the Report — of Lady Brittle's Intrigue — with Capt Boastall —

Spat — Madam by this Lady Brittle is the talk of half the Town — & in a week — will be toasted as a demirep —

Mrs Sneerwell. What have you done as to the innuendo — of Miss Niceby's fondness for her own Footman —

Spatter — 'Tis in a fine train ma'am — I told it to my Hair-Dresser — he courts a milleners girl in Pall-Mall whose mistress has a first Cousin — who is waitwoman to Lady Clackit — I think in about fourteen hours — it must reach Lady Clackit — & then you know the Business is done —

Mr S. — But is that sufficient do you think?

Spatter I led Madam — I'll undertake to ruin the Character of the premier prude in London with half as much — ha! ha! did you never hear how poor Miss Wortley — lost her lover — & her character — last summer at Scarborough — & this was the whole — of it — one Evening at Lady Seringer's the conversation happen'd to turn on — the Difficulty — of breeding nova Scotia Sheep in England. I have known instances says — says Miss Louther —

for last a spring a Friend of mine — miss Shepherd
of Rams-Gate — had — a Nova-Scotia — Sheep that produced her Twins — what cries the old deaf dowager
Baulwell — has Miss Shep[h]erd of Ramsgate been
brought to bed of Twins — ? — this mistake
as you may suppose set the Company a laughing — However — the next
Day — Miss — Verjuice Amarila Lonely[?] — who had been
of the Party — talking of Lady Baulwells Deafness — began
to tell what had happened — but unluckily for-
getting to say a word of the Sheep — it was
understood — by the company — and in every circle — many
beleived — that Miss Shepherd of Ramsgate
had actually been brought to bed of a fine Boy
and a Girl, and in less than a Fortnight there were People who could
name the Father, and the Farm-House where the Babies were put
— out to Nurse. —

Mrs S.	Ha! ha! — well for a Stroke of Luck it was a very good one — I suppose — you find no difficulty — in spreading the Report on the censorious Miss
Spatter.	none in the world — she has always been so ~~haught~~ prudent and ~~sly~~ reserved — that every body — was sure there was some Reason for it at Botom. —
Mrs [S.]	Yes — a Tale of Scandal is as fatal to the Credit of — a Prude as a Fever to those of the Strongest Constitution — but there is a sort of sickly Reputation — that outlive[s] hundred[s] of the robuster Character of a Prude —
Spatter —	True Maam there are Valetudinarians in Reputation as in Consti[t]utions — and and both are cautious from their appreciation and consciousness of their weak side — and avoid the least breath of air

for last a Spring a Friend of mine — Miss Shepherd
of Ramsgate — had — a Nova-Scotia-Sheep that pro
:duced her Twins — what was the old deaf Dowager
Boulmell — has Miss Shepherd of Ramsgate been
brought to bed of Twins —? — this mistake
set the Company a laughing — however — — the next
Day — Miss Venge's Amanda surely — who had been
of the Party — talking of Lady Boulmell, — began
to tell being ill-informed — but unluckily for
:getting to say a word of the Sheep — it was
understood — by the company — & every — every
believed — that Miss Shepherd of Ramsgate
had been brought to bed of — a fine Boy
& a Girl & in less than a fortnight there were People who could
name the Father of the Poor House where the Babies were put
out to Nurse —

Mr. S. Ha! ha! — well for a stock of such it was a
very good one — — I suppose — you find no difficulty —
in spreading the Watch on the censorious Miss

Spatter. none in the world — she has always been so prudish
and reserved — that every body — was sure there was
some Reason for it at Bottom. —

Mr. Yes — a Tale of Scandal is as fatal to the Credit of — a Prude
as a Fever to those of the Strongest Constitution — but there
is a sort of sickly Reputation — that outlive hundred of the
robustest Character of a Prude —

Spatter. True because there are Valetudinarians in Reputation as
in Constitution — and and both are cautious from their
apprehensive consciousness of their own side — & avoid
the least breath of air

23

Lady. Sneerwell.	But Spatter — I have something of greater Confidence now to entrust you with — I think I have some claim to your Gratitude —
Spatter —	Have I ever shewn — myself one moment unconscious of what I owe You —
Mrs S.	I do not charge you with it — but this is an affair of importance — You are acquainted with my Situation — but not all my weaknesses — I was Hurt in the early Part of my Life but[sic] the envenom'd Tongue of Scandal — and ever since I own I have no joy but in sullying the Fame of others which I could not keep — in this I have found you an apt Tool — you have often been the instrument of my Revenge — but you must now assist me in a softer Passion — A young — Widow with a Title and a larg[e] Fortune is seldom driven — to sue — yet is that my case — of the many you [have] seen here have you ever observ'd — me secretly — to favour one —
Spat—	Egad — I never was more pozed — I'm sure you — can not mean — that ridiculous old Knight Sr Christopher Crab —
Lady S.	A wretch — his Assiduities are my Torment —
[Spat.]	Perhaps — his Nephew the Baronet — Sr Benjamin Backbite is the happy man —
Mrs S.	No — tho' He has ill nature — and a good Person on his

24

Lady-Sneerwell. But Spatter - I have something of greater con=
=fidence now to entrust you with -- I think I have some
claim to your Gratitude -

Spatter - Have I ever shewn - myself one moment unconsci=
=ious of what I owe you -

Mrs S. I don't charge you with it - but this is an affair
of importance -- You are acquainted with my
situation - but not all my weaknesses - I was
hurt in the early Part of my Life but the envenom'd
Tongue of Scandal - and ever since I own I have
no joy but in sullying the fame of others which
I could not keep - in this I have found you
an apt Tool - you have often been the instrument
of my Revenge - but you must now spirit me in a
softer Passion - A young - widow with a title & a long
Fortune is seldom discreet to me - yet is that my case -
of the many you seen here have you ever ob=
=serv'd - me seemingly - to favour one -

Spat - Egad - I never was more posed - I'm sure
you - can not mean - that ridiculous old thing
Sr Christopher Crab -

Lady S. A conceited - his asperities are my Torment -

. Brother - his Nephew the Baronet - Sr Benjamin
Backbite is the happy man -

Lady S. No - tho' He has ill nature - 2 a good Person on his

	side — He is not to my taste. — what — think you of Clerimont?
Spatter.	How — the profess'd Lover of your Ward — Maria — between whom too — there is a mutual Affection —
Mrs S.	Yes that Insensible! — that Dotes on an Idiot is the Man —
Spatter	But how can you hope to succeed —
[Lady S.]	By Poisoning — both with Jealousy of the Other — 'till the Credulous Fool in a Pique shall be entangled in my Snare —
Spat	Have you taken any measure for it —
[Lady S.]	I have — Maria has made me the Confidante of Clerimonts Love for her — in return I pretended to entrust [her] with my affection for Sr Benjamin — who is her warm admirer — by strong representation of my Passion I prevailed on her not to refuse — to see Sr Benj. whi[c]h she once promised Clerimont to do — I entreaded [sic] her to plead my cause — and even drew — her in to answer Sr Benjamins Letters — with the same intent — of this I have made Clerimont Suspicious — but 'tis you must — inflame him to the Pitch I want. —
Spatter—	But will not Maria — on the least unkindness ~~of~~ from Clerimont — instantly come to an explanation
Mrs S.	this is what we must prevent~~ed~~ — by blinding

side - He is not to my taste . — what
think you of Clermont —

Lucretia How — the profess'd Lover of your Ward. Maria —
between whom 'tis — there is a mutual Affection .

Wm. Yes that Insensible ! — that Dotes on an Idiot is
the Mean —

Lucretia But how can you hope to succeed —

By Poisoning — both with Jealousy of the Other — till
the Credulous Fool in a Pique shall be entangled in
my Snare —

Lucretia Have you taken any measure for it —

I have — Maria has made me the Confidente
of Clermont's Love for her — in return I pretended
to entrust with my affection for Sr Benjamin —
who he is her warm admirer — by strong mis =
= presentation of my Passion I prevailed on her
not to refuse — to see Sr Benj. which she once
promised Clermont to do — — I intended her to
plead my cause — & even drew her in to an =
= swer Sr Benjamins Letters . with the same intent — of
this I have made Clermont suspicious — but to you
must . inflame him to the Pitch I want . —

Lucretia — But will not Maria — or the least mischief upon
Clermont — instantly come to an explanation

Wm. this is what we must prevent — by blinding

her equally with regard — to Clerimont —

Sp.   who can you //~~Lady~~// make ~~me~~ her jealous of
perhaps of myself — but that must be
as circumstances arise — but hold I hear
her coming —

Spat.   well I'll leave you for a while — I promised
to call on Sr Christopher this morning — and I'll
return presently for further Instructions.

— Enter Maria —

Lady S.   Well my Love — have you seen — Clerimont to Day? —

Mar.   I have not — nor does He come so often as He used — indeed Madam
I fear — what I have done to serve you — has by some means come to
his Knowledge — and injured me in his Knowledge — as I promised
him faithfully never to see Sr Benjamin — what confidence
can He ever have in me if He once finds I have broken my
word to him —

Lady S.   Nay you are too grave — if He should suspect anything it will always be in my Power to undeceive him

M.   Well you have involved me in Deceit — and I must trust to you
to ~~execute~~ extricate me.

L.S.   Have — you answerd Sr Benjamins last Letter in the manner
I wish'd —

M.   I have written exactly as you desired me — but I wish you
would give me leave — to tell the whole Truth to Clerimont at once: there is a Coldness in his manner of

28

her equally with regard to Clevimont —

M. who can you make her jealous of
perhaps of myself — but that must be
as circumstances arise — but hold I hear
her coming —

Srob. well I'll leave you for a while — I promised
to call on S. Charles Euba this morning — & I'll
return presently for farther instructions —
————— Extr Maria —————

Lady L. Well my Love — have you seen Clevimont to Day? —
Mar. I have not — nor does He come so often as He used — indeed madam
I fear what I have done to serve you — has by some means come to
his Knowledge — & injured me in his Knowledge — — I promised
him faithfully never to see S. Benjamin — what confidence
can He ever have in me if He once finds I have broken my
word to him —

Lady L. Nay you are too grave — if He should suspect any
thing it will always be in my Power to undeceive him

M. Well you have involved me in Deceit — I must trust to you
to extricate me.

L.L. Have — you answer'd S. Benjamins last Letter in the manner
I wish'd —

M. I have written exactly as you desired me — but I wish you
would give me leave — to tell the whole Touth to Clevimont at once; there is a coldness in his manner of

Late which I can no ways account for —

L.S.   Im glad to find I have work'd on him so far —
fie! Maria — have you so little regard for me?
would you put me to the Shame of being known
to Love a Man who disregards me — had you entrusted me with such a Secret — not a Husbands
Power should have forced it from me! but
do as you please — go — forget the Affection
I have shewn you — forget that I have been
as a mother to you whom I found an orphan —
go break thro' all ties of gratitude and expose
me to the worlds — Derision to avoid one sullen Hour
from a moody Lover.

M.   Indeed Madam — you wrong me — and — you who know
the Apprehension of Love — should make allowance
for it's weakness — my Love for Clerimont is so great —

L.S.   Peace it cannot — exceed mine —

M.   For Sr Benjamin — perhaps not maam — and I am sure
Clerimont's has as sincere an Affection for me —

[L.S.]   Would to Heavu'n I could say the same!

[M.]   Of Sr Benjamin! — I wish so too Maam — but I am sure
you would be extremely hurt — if in gaining your wishes
you were to injure me in the opinion of Clerimont

late which I can no ways account for ...

L.S.   I'm glad to find I have work'd on him so far -
Fie! Maria - have you so little regard for me?
would you put me to the shame of being known
to love a man who disregards me - had you en=
=trusted me with such a secret - not a Husbands
Power should have forced it from me: but
do as you please - go - forget the Affection
I have shewn you - forget that I have been
as a mother to you whom I found an orphan -
go break thro' all ties of gratitude & expose
me to the worlds Derision to avoid one sullen Hour
from a moody Lover.

M.   Indeed Madam - you wrong me - & - you who know
the Apprehension of Love - should make allowance
for it's weakness - my Love for Clermont is so great -

C.S.   Peace it cannot - exceed mine -

M.   Nor Sr Benjamin - perhaps not Madam - & I am sure
Clermont has as sincere an Affection for me -
Would to Heav'n I could say the same!

Of Sr Benjamin! - I wish so too Madam - but I am sure
you would be extremely hurt - if in gaining your wishes
you were to injure me in the opinion of Clermont

L.S.	Undoubtedly — I would not for the world — simple Fool — but my wishes — my Happiness depends on you — for I doat so — on this insensible — that it kills me to see him so attach'd you — give me but Clerimont — and —
M.	Clerimont!
L.S.	Sr Benjamin — you know I mean — is He not attach'd to you — am I not slighted for you — yet do I bear any Enmity to you as I[sic] rival — I only request your Friendly intercession and you are so ungrateful you would deny me that.

⟨do you call this so great a Piece of service?
The greatest — when I did wrong to oblige you I did the utmost.⟩

M.	Nay Madam — have I not done Everything you wish'd — for you I have departed from Truth — and contaminated my mind with Falsehood ~~to serve you~~ — what could I do more to serve you.
L.S.	Well — forgive me — I was — too warm — I know — you would not betray me — well — I expect Sr Benjamin and his Unckle this morning — why Maria do you always leave our little Parties —
M	I own Madam — I have no Pleasure in their Conversation — I have myself no gratification in uttering Detraction and therefore none in hearing —
L.S.	O fie! you are too Serious — 'tis only a little harmless Raillery —
M.	I never can think that Harmless — which hurts the Peace — of Youth — draws tears from Beauty — and gives many a Pang to the Innocent —

3

L.P. Undoubtedly — I would not for the world — simple Fool. but my wishe — my Happiness depends on you — for I doat so — on these insensible — that it kills me to see them so attach'd you — give me but Clermont — 2 —

M. Clermont !

L.S. S.ʳ Benjamin — you know I mean — is she not attach'd to you — am I not slighted for you — yet do I bear any Enmity to you as I rival — I only request your Friendly in- terception, & you are so ungrateful you would deny me that. do you call this so great a Piece of service? The greatest — when I did wrong to oblige you I did the utmost.

M. Nay Madam — have I not done Everything you wish'd — for you I have departed from Truth — & contaminated my mind with Falsehood to serve you — what could I do more to serve you.

L.S. Well — forgive me — I was — too warm — I know — you would not betray me — — well — I expect S.ʳ Benjamin & his Uncle this morning — pray maria do you always leave our little Parties —

M. I own Madam — I have no Pleasure in their Conversation — I have myself no gratification in uttering Detraction & therefore none in hearing —

L.S. O fie! you are too Serious — 'tis only a little harmless Raillery —

M. I never can think that Harmless — which hurts the Peace — of youth — draws tear from Beauty — and gives wrong sting to the Innocent —

[L.S.]	nay you must allow that many People of sense and wit have this Foible — Sr Benjamin Backbite for Instance —
M.	He may perhaps — but I confess I never can perceive wit where I see malice —
L.S.	Fie Maria — you have the most unpolish'd way of Thinking! it is absolutely impossible to be witty without being a little ill natur'd — the malice of a good thing is the barb that make[s] it stick — I protest now when I say an illnatured thing — I have not the least malice against the Person — and indeed it may be of one whom I never saw in my Life — for I hate to abuse a Friend but I take it for granted they all speak — as ill naturedly of me —
M.	Then you very probably — are conscious you deserve it — for my Part I do //shall// not suppose myself ill spoken of — when I am conscious I deserve it. —

Enter Serv—

[Serv.]	Mrs Candour —
M.	well I'll leave you —
L.S.	No — No — ~~I'll~~ Sure — you have no reason to avoid her She is goodnature itself —
M.	Yes — with an artful Affectation of Candour — she does more Injury than the worst Bac[k]biter of them all —

Enter Mrs Candour —

Mrs C.	So — Lady Sneerwell — how d'ye do! Maria — Child —

25

way you must allow that many People of sense & wit have this foible — Sr Benjamin Backbite for instance —

M. He may perhaps — but I confess I never can perceive wit where I see malice —

L.S. Psha Maria — you have the most unpolish'd way of Thinking! it is absolutely impossible to be witty without being a little ill natur'd — the malice of a good thing is the barb that make it stick — I protest now when I say an illnatured thing — I have not the least malice against the Person — & indeed it may be of one whom I never saw in my life — for I hate to abuse a Friend but I take it for granted they all speak — or ill acting of me —

M. Then you very probably are conscious you deserve it — for my Part I do surely not suppose myself ill spoken of — when I am conscious I deserve it. —

Enter Serv. — Mrs Candour —

M. — well I'll leave you —

Ld. No. No. — I love you — you have no reason to avoid her She is goodnature itself —

Sr — Yes — with an artful affectation of Candour — she does more Injury than the worst practiser of them all —

Exit Mrs Candour —

Mrs. So — Lady Sneerwell — how dye do! Maria — Child —

how dos't? — well who is't you are to marry at last —
~~the world talks~~ Sr Benjamen — and Clerimont — the Town
talks of nothing else —

[M.]   I'm very sorry ma'am the Town has so little to do —

Mrs C.   true! true! Child but there is no stopping Peoples' Mouths
why it was but this morning that I heard Miss Gadabout —
had — elope'd with Sir Filigree Flird [sic] — but Lud! there is no
~~belie~~ mind[ing] what People say — some Folks are so
fond of Chattering — last week it was currently reported
that Lord Buffalo — had discover'd my Lady ~~and~~ in Bagnio —
but when the truth — came out — Lord it was nothing
but an act of Charity to a poor Girl — who lay dying there
in a Fever!

⟨The fever goal   Another [?]⟩

[M.]   Such reports are highly Scandalous —

[Mrs C.]   So they are Child — shameful — shameful — but
[what] can be done — the world is so censorious the smallest
matter affords a Scandal — Lord — who would
ever have ~~spe~~ suspected Miss Musgriny[?] of an Intrigue
yet so illnatured is the world — they will have it now —
that her Dropsy was only a nine months Disorder — isn't
this monstrous!

M.   'Tis indeed — but I think they who report
such things are equally culpable —

has do'it? — well who is't you are to marry at last —
the world talks ~~~~~ S:r Benjamin — a Clerimont — the Town
talks of nothing else —

I'm very sorry ma'am the Town has so little to do —
M:rs — tone! tone! Child! but there is no stopping People's mouths —
why it was but this morning that I heard Miss Gadabout
had elop'd with S:r Filigree Flirt — but Lud! there is no
minding what People say — some Folks are so
fond of Chattering — last week it was currently reported
that Lord Buffalo had discover'd my Lady of Bagnio —
but when the truth came out — Lord! it was nothing
but an act of Charity to a poor Girl — who lay dying there
in a Fever!
the face some
Author
Such reports are highly Scandalous —
So they are Child — — shameful — shameful — — but
can't be done — the world is so censorious the smallest
matter affords a Handle — Lord — who who would
ever have suspected Miss Languish of an Intrigue
yet so illnatured is the world — they will have it now
that her Dropsy was only a nine months Disorder — is n't
this monstrous!
'Tis indeed — but I think they who report
such things are equally culpable —

Mrs C.   Very true! — that was always my Opinion
                The — Tale-Bearers — as I have said an hundred
                times — the tale-Bearers are as bad as the Tale
                Makers — that's my maxim — ~~yester~~ to day
                Lady Clackit told me that Mr and Mrs ——
                did not agree so well as they used — and
                she likewise expected that a certain Lady
                in not an hundred miles from Soho's [~~illegible~~]
                whose name I don't chuse to mention —
                had — been detected in a Correspondence with a
                certain Captain — and she also added that Miss
                — etc. — but do you think I would
                report these Things — no — no — the Tale -
                Bearers as I said before are as bad as the
                Tale-makers — well — but Child tell
                me now — when are you to be married —
                what! I warrant Sr Benjamin is to be the
                Man after all! well ~~If~~ Sr Benjamin is a very fine
                Gentleman —

[M.]   Indeed Ma'am you are wrong.

[Mrs C.]   What then tis Clerimont — is a very pretty Gentleman and
                I dare swear the Report of his ~~Engagement~~ being con-
                tracted to a Lady in Norfolk — is entirely without
                foundation. —

M.C. Very true! — that was always my Opinion — The — Tale-Bearers — as I have said an hundred times — the tale-Bearers are as bad as the false Speakers — that's my maxim — why to day had Clarbet told me that Mr & Mrs ———— did not agree so well as they used — and she likewise asserted that a certain Lady in not an hundred miles from ———— whose name I don't chuse to mention — had been detected in a correspondence with a certain Captain — & she also added that Miss ———— — but do you think I would report these Things — no — no — the Tale- -Bearers as I said before are as bad as the Tale-makers — — will — but Child tell me now — when are you to be married — what! I warrant D? Benjamin is to be the Man after all! well H? D? Benjamin is a very fine Gentleman —

Indeed M'am you are wrong.

What then Mr Clement — is a very pretty Gentleman & I dare swear the Report of his Engagement being con = = tracted to a Lady in Norfolk — is entirely without foundation. —

M.	How Ma'am — contracted?
Mrs C.	Lud! Child I suppose you are no stranger to the Business! — but perhaps there may be nothing in it — to be sure I have heard the Lady's name and that from the best authority — but there is [no] knowing! What did you never hear of it —
[M.]	Why Ma'am I have suspected —
[Mrs C.]	but Child don't let it vex you — it may not be true — tho' Men are sad Deceivers —

Enter Lad S.

L.S.	Dear Mrs Candour — I beg your Pardon — Maria what's the matter —
[Mrs C.]	I was only mentioning an old report of Clerimont ['s] affair with a Lady in Norfolk —
[L.S.]	O that's an old Business — lately miscarried —
[M.]	Indeed Ma'am — so then perhaps this is the Cause of Clerimont's unkindness —
[L.S.]	Mrs Candour give me leave — to speak to you

Enter Serv.

M.   How Ma'am – contracted?

M^{rs}C.   Lord! Child I suppose you are no stranger to
        the Business! – – but perhaps there may be nothing
        in it – to be sure I have heard the Lady's name
        & that from ye best authority – but there is knowing
        what did you never hear of it –
        Why Ma'am I have suspected –
        but Child don't let it vex you – it may not be true.
        tho' men are sad Deceivers – –

Enter Lad S.

S.   Dear Mrs Candour – I beg your Pardon – – Ma'am what's
        the matter –
        I was only mentioning an old report of Clermont's
        affair with a Lady in Norfolk –
        O that an old Business – lately revived –
        Indeed Ma'am – so they perhaps; this is the
        Cause of Clermont's unkindness – Mrs Candour
        give me leave – to speak to you

Ex^t Serv.

Sr C.	⟨I'm very glad you think so
Mrs S.	Nay — She has charming Fresh Colour —
Sr C.	Yes when tis fresh put on —

Destinies — in Tapestry —

the most intrepid Blush — I have seen her complection
stand fire for an hour together!

Lad S.	No — no — 'tis n't that she paints ill but then —
	and I'll be judge'd by her Face —
	She is the worst artist and I would say it to her Face —
	would you say this to her Face —
	Which Face — ⟩

Sr. P.   I'm very glad you think so

Mrs. Nov — She has charming Fresh Colour —

Sr. P. — Yes when 'tis fresh put on —

Dublin in Tapestry —

X the most interesting Blush — I have seen her complection
stand fire for an hour together —

Ld. S.   No, no — 'tis n't that she paints ill but then —
                    I'll be judge'd by her Face —
She is the worst artist & I would say it to her Face ---
would you say this to her Face —
Which Face —

43

Mrs S.	Now I'll die but you are so scandalous I'll for-swear your Society — sure you must confess our Friend Lady Carmine — is really Beautiful —
~~Sr B.~~	~~Who Lady Carmine! o Lud! o Lud!~~
Mrs S.	Nay ~~she has~~ it is truly delicate ~~Complection~~ Bloom
Sr B.	Yes 'tis a truly delicate indeed — for 'twould bear handling no more than the Bloom of Plum —
Mrs S.	O fie I swear 'tis natural — I've seen it come and go —
Sr C.	I dare swear you have — it comes //goes// ~~of an evening~~ Night and comes again in the morning —
Sr B.	— true — Sr Christopher — it not only comes and goes but what's more her maid can fetch and carry it —
Mrs S.	Ha! ha! ha! — how I hate to hear you talk so but sure — her Sister Lady Stucco — is or *was* a very fine Woman —
Sr C.	Who Lady Stucco — o Lud! — She's six and fifty if she's an Hour —
Mrs S.	Nay positively you wrong her — fifty two or fifty three is the Utmost —
Sr C.	But then — zounds she lays it on thicker than her ~~Aunt~~ Sister —
Sr P [sic]	So she does I'll swear — and when she has finish'd her Face she joins it so badly to her Neck — that she looks like a mended statue in which the connisseur sees at once that the Heads modern tho' the ~~Hands~~ Trunk's antique — ⟨Here's such scandal about Painting⟩

44

9

Mrs. S. Now I'll die but you are so scandalous I'll for=
swear your society — you must confess our
Friend Lady Carmine — is really Beautiful —

Sir B. ~~Who Lady Carmine! — absolutely such~~

Mrs. S. Nay she has truly delicate Complection Bloom

Sir B. yes 'tis a truly delicate indeed — for 'twould bear
handling no more than the Bloom of a Plum —

Mrs. S. O fie I swear 'tis natural — I've seen it come &
go —

Sir C. I dare swear you have — it comes of a Night
& comes again in the morning —

Sir B. — true — Mrs. Evergreen — it not only comes & goes but
her maid can fetch & carry it. — while more

Mrs. S. Ha! ha! ha! — how I hate to hear you talk so.
but sure — her Sister Lady Stucco — is or was a very
fine woman —
                    Stucco
Sir C. Who Lady — a head! — she's fifty if she's an hour —

Mrs. S. Nay positively you wrong her — fifty two or fifty three is
the Utmost —

Sir C. But then — sure the lays it on thicker than her Sister

Sir P. So she does I'll swear — and when she has finish'd
her Face she joins it so badly to her Neck — that she
looks like a mended statue in which the connoisseur
sees at once that the Heads modern tho' the
Trunk's antique —

        Here's such scandal about Painting

⟨Lady Moral — to hear Lady Stucco talk Sentiments
        Like French Fruit made up
of Paint and Proverbs —

if Friend is to ~~suffer~~ be attack'd they suffer
for some time ~~but~~ from thinking[?] — but they never
thoroughly loose their Character 'till Candour takes
their Part. may I be attack'd by you
every Day and worse still may Mrs Candour
take my Part. —

        Nay Pray Mrs. Candour don't take
his Part — He is a Friend of mine
and I should be very sorry for him to lose
his Character — ⟩

10

Lady Moral - to hear Lady Stucco talk Sentiment
Like French Fruit made up
of Paint & Proverbs --

if Friend is to ~suffer~ be attach'd they suffer
for some time ~but~ from them - but they never
thoroughly loose their Character 'till Candour takes
their Part - may I be attach'd by you
every Day & never still may Mrs Candour
takes my Part -

Nay, Pray Mrs Candour don't take
his Part - He is a Friend of mine
& I should be very sorry for him to loose
his Character --

Mrs S.	Ha! ha! well you make me laugh — but I swear I hate you for it — what do you think of Miss Simper?
Sr B.	Why she has very pretty Teeth —
Sr C.	Yes and on that account when she is neither speaking or — Laughing (which very seldom happens) she never absolutely shuts her mouth bu[.] ¹eaves it on a jar as it were—
Mrs S.	How can you be so ill natured —for sure even thats — better — than to be at the Pains Lady Prim takes to conceal her losses — she has drawn in her mouth 'till it absolutely resembles the Aperture of a Poor's Box — and all her words appear to slide out edgeways —
Sr B.	— Wery[sic] well Mrs Sneerwell — I see you can be a little severe —
Mrs S.	In defence of a Friend — 'tis but Justice — but you are so scandalous you allow good qualities to no one — not even good nature to my Friend Mrs Pursy —
Sr [B.]	What the old fat widow of Hanover-square — ?
Mrs S.	Nay that's her misfortune — and I'm sure when she takes such pains to get rid of it no one should reflect on her —
Mrs S.[sic]	true — true —
Mrs S.	She almost — lives on acids and small whey — laces herself in Pullies — and then in Summer — at the hottest hour of Noon — you may see her take the air — or rather taking the Dust in high Park — with her Hair plaited like a Foot Soldier — on a little squat Poney that trots like a Coach Horse —
Sr C.	Well said Mrs. Sneerwell — I see you wont excuse her
Mrs S.	Well then when the poor woman takes such Pains you should not ridicule her — but you are as sensorious — as Miss Saunter —
Sr. B.	Yes — and she is a curious creature to pretend to be

Mrs. S. — Ha! ha! well you make me laugh — but I swear I hate you for it — — what do you think of Miss Simper?

P.B. — Why she has very pretty Teeth —

T.C. — Yes & on that account when she is neither speaking or laughing (which very seldom happens) she never absolutely shuts her mouth, but leaves it on a jar as it were —

Mrs. S. — How can you be so ill natured — for sure even that's better — than to be at the Pains Lady Owen takes to conceal her lips — she has drawn in her mouth 'till it absolutely resembles the aperture of a Poor's Box — & all her words appear to slide out edgeways — —

P.B. — — Very well Mrs. Surewell I see you can be a little severe —

Mrs. S. — In defence of a Friend 'tis but Justice — but you are so scandalous you allow good qualities to no one — not even good nature to my Friend Mrs Pursy — —

J: — What the old fat widow of Hanover — severe —?

Mrs. S — Nay that's her misfortune — & I'm sure when she takes such pains to get rid of it no one should reflect on her —

Mrs. S. — true — true —

Mrs. S. — She almost lives on acids & small whey — laces herself in Bullies — and then in Summer — at the hottest hour of Noon — you may see her taking the air on foot together taking the Dust in high Park — on a little sweat Poney that looks like a coach Horse — — —

P.C. — Well said Mrs Surewell — I see you would excuse her —

Mrs. S. — Well then when the poor woman takes such Pains you should not ridicule her — but you are as censorious as Mrs Saunter —

P.B. — Yes — & she is a curious creature to pretend to be

⟨Charards[sic] — my First — is —

L.S.   I believe scandalous stories ~~are~~ never rise —
without some Foundation — ⟩

12

Chenewold — my Fred — is —

S. J. I believe scandalous stories ~~are~~ never rise—
without some foundation ———

censorious —

[Sr C.]   Who Lady — Saunter — the gawky awkward without any
one good quality under Heaven —

Mrs S.   Positively you shall not be so abusive — ~~you~~ she Lady
Saunter is a near relation of mine by marriage — as for her
Person — indeed great allowance is to be made — a
woman — labou[r]s under great disadvantages when she's
tries to pass for a Girl at six and thirty — tho' surely
she *is* handsome still — the weakness in her Eyes — considering how much she reads by Candlelight is not to be
wonder'd at — and as for her manner — upon my word
I think 'tis particularly graceful considering she never
had the least Education — for you know her mother was
a welch millener and her Father a Sugar Baker — in Bristol.

Sr C.   Ah you are to[o] good natured Lady Sneerwell —

Mrs S.   I own I cannot bear to hear my Friends ill spoken of —
when they have failing[s] I love to be blind — and so I always
told — my Cousin — Saunter — and you know what pretensions
she has to be critical in! —

S.B.   O to be sure she has the oddest Face
⟨Table Dot — at Spaw whose Features repainted⟩
— a collection of a
Feature from — all different countries — an Irish front — a
Dutch nose //comp[lection] of a Spainard //— sallow french Face, Teeth
    all Chainous — in short
her Face resembles a Congress at the close of a general War
where all the members — even to her Eyes have a different
Interest, while her Nose and Chin are the only parties likely
to join issue —

Sr B.[sic]   Go you are a provoking Toad —

censorious —

who Lady — Sneerwell — the ...... without any
one good quality under Heaven —

M: S.   Positively you shall not be so abusive ... Lady
Saunter is a near relation of mine *by marriage* — as for her
Person — indeed great allowance is to be made — a
woman — labours under great disadvantages when she's
trying to pass for a Girl at six & thirty — tho' surely
she is handsome still — the weakness in her Eyes — consi=
=dering how much she reads by candlelight is not to be
wonder'd at — and as for her manner — upon my word
I think it's particularly graceful considering she never
had the least Education — for you know her mother was
a welsh milliner & her Father a Sugar Baker — in Bristol —

J: C.   Ah you are too good natured Lady Sneerwell —

M: S.   I own I cannot bear to hear my friends ill spoken of —
where they have failings I love to be be blind — & so I always
told — my cousin — Saunter — & you know what pretensions
she has to be centered in —

S: B.   O to be sure she has the oddest Face — a collection of a
Feature from all different countries — an Irish front — a
Dutch nose — ... French ... teeth all Chinese — — in short
her Face resembles a congress at the close of a general War
where all the members — even to her Eyes have a different
Interest, while her Nose & Chin are the only parties likely
to join issue —

C: R.   So you are a good-natured friend —

Enter Clerimont —

This Clerimont is to be sure the drollest Mortal! He is one of your moral Fellows — who does unto others as He would they should do unto him —

L.S.   Yet He is sometimes Entertaining

Sr C.   Oh hang him — no — He has too much //dull// good Nature to say a witty thing himself — and too illnatur'd — to praise wit in others. —

Sr B.   So Clerimont! we were just wishing for you to enliven us with your wit and agreeable Vein. —

Cl.   No Sr Benjamin I cannot join you —

Sr B.   Why Man you look — as grave — as A young Lover ~~when~~ the first time He's jilted —

[Cl.]   I have — some cause to be grave — Sr Benjamin a word with you — (and all) I have just received a Letter from the Country — in which I understand that my Sister has suddenly left my Unkle's House and has not since been heard of —

L.S.   Indeed — and on what Provocation —

C.   It seem's they were urging her a little too harshly to marry — some country Squire that was not to her Taste

Sr B.   Positively I love her for her Spirit —

L.S.   and so do I and would protect her too — if I knew where she was —

Enter Clervmont –

This Clervmont is to be sure the dullest Mortal! He is one of your moral Fellows – who does unto others as He would they should do unto him –

L.S. Yet He is sometimes Entertaining

T.C. Oh hang him – no – He has too much good Natured to say a witty thing himself – & too ill natur'd. to praise wit in others. – –

S.B. So Clervmont! we were just wishing for you to enliven us with your wit & agreeable Vein. –

Cl. – No Sir Benjamin I cannot join you –

S.B. Why then you look as grave – as A young Lover the first time He's jilted – –
I have some cause to be grave – Sir Benjamin a word with you – (aside) I have just received a Letter from the Country – in which I understand that my Sister has suddenly left my Uncles' House & has not since been heard of –

J.S. Indeed – a on what Provocation –

Cl. It seem's they were urging her a little too harshly to marry – some country 'squire that was not to her Taste

S.B. – Positively I love her for her Spirit –

J.S. & so do I & would protect her too – if I knew where she was –

Cle.	Sr Benjamin a word — with you — I think Sr we have lived for some years on [what] the world calls the footing of Friends —
[Sr B.]	To my great Honour — Sir — well my dear Friend —
[Cl.]	You know that you on[c]e paid your address[es] to my Sister — my Unckle disliked you but I have — reason to think — you were not indifferent to her —
[Sr B.]	I beleive you are pretty right there but what follows —
[Cl.]	Then I think I have [a] right to ex~~plain~~ect an implicit Answer from you whether you are in any respect — privy to her Elopement. —
[Sr. B.]	Why you certainly have a right to ask the Question — and I will answer you as sin- cerely — which is that tho' I make no doubt but that she would have gone with me to the worlds end — I am at present entirely ignorant of the whole Affair — this I declare to you upon my Honour. —

56

Ch. — S.r Benjamin a word with you — I think
S.r we have lived for some years on
the world calls the footing of Friends —
To my great Honour — Sir — with my dear
Friend —

You know that you once paid your addresses
to my Sister — my Uncle disbelieved us
but I have — reason to think — you
were not indifferent to her —

I believe you are pretty right there but
what follows —

Then I think I have right to expect
an explicit Answer from you whether
you are in any respect — privy to
her Elopement . —

Why you certainly have a right to ask
the Question — & I will answer you sin=
:cerely — which is that tho' I make no
doubt, but that she would have gone
with me to the world's end — I am
at present entirely ignorant of the
whole Affair — this I declare to
you upon my Honour . —

and what is more I assure you my Devotions
are at present paid to another Lady — one
of your acquaintance too —

C.   Now! who can this other be whom He alludes to
— I have sometimes thought I perceived a kind
of mistery between him and Maria — but I rely
on her Promise — tho' of Late her Conduct to
me has been Strangely reserved! —

L.S.   Why Clerimont — you seem quite thoughtful —
come — with us we are going to kill an hour
at Kings[?] — your mistress will join us ~~there~~

C.   Madam — I attend you —   *ex* —

L.S.   Sr Benjamin — I see Maria is now coming
to join us — do you detain — [her] here a while
and I will contrive that Clerimont should see you
and then drop this Letter —
                                   exe —

— Enter Maria —

[M.]   I thought the Company were here — and Clerimont

Sr B.   One more your Slave than Clerimont is here —

[M.]   Dear Sr B. I thought you promised me to drop this
Subject — if I have really any Power over you
you will oblige me —

& what is more I assure you any Devotion are at present paid to another Ledy – one of your acquaintance too –

C. Now! who can this other be whom He alludes to – I have sometimes thought I perceived a kind of mistery between him & maria – but I rely on her Promise – this of late her conduct to me has been Strangely reserved! –

J.J. Why Clerimont – you seem quite thoughtful – come – with us we are going to Call on Four at Shine – your mistriss will join us the

C. Madam I attend you – ex –

J.J. S:r Benjamin – I see Maria is now coming to join us – do you detain – beau a while & I will contrive that Clerimont should see you – & then drop this letter –

exe –

– Enter Maria –

I thought the Company were here – & Clerimont

S:B. One more your Slave than Clerimont is here – Dear S:B. I thought you promised me to drop this Subject – if I have really any Power over you you will oblige me – – –

[Sr B.]	Power over me! what is there you could not command me in! — have you not wrought on me — to proffer my Love — to Lady S. — yet tho' you — gain this from me you will not give me the smallest token of gratitude!

Enter Cler. and Lad. S.

M.	How can I beleive your Love sincere when you continue still to importune me —
[Sr B.]	I ask but for your Friendship your Esteem —
[M.]	That you shall ever be entitled to! — then I may depend upon your honour —
[Sr B.]	Eternally — dispose of my Heart — as you please ~~I may dispose of~~
[M.]	Depend on't I shall study nothing but it's Happiness I need not repeat — my Caution — as to Clerimont —
[Sr B.]	No — no He suspects nothing as yet. —
[M.]	For within this[sic] few Days I ~~supposed~~ almost beleived that He suspected me —
[Sr B.]	Never fear — He does not love well enough to be quick-sighted — for He just now He tax'd me with eloping with his Sister —
[M.]	Well we had now best join the Company. *exe —*
Cl.	So! — who now can ever have faith in Women —

60

Power over me! what is there you could not
command me in! — have you not wrought
on me — to proffer my Love — to Lady S. — yet
tho' you — gain that from me you will not
give me the smallest token of gratitude! —

M. How can I believe your Love sincere when
^(enter Bev. & Lad. S.)
you continue still to importune me —
I ask but for your Friendship your esteem —
That you shall ever be entitled to — then
I may depend upon your honour —
Eternally — — dispose of my Heart — or you please —
~~you dispose~~
Depend on't I shall study nothing but its Happiness
I need ^not repeat — my Caution — as to Clerimont —
No — ^s he suspects nothing as yet —
For within this few Days I ~~supposed~~ almost
believ'd that he suspected me —
Never fear — He does not love well enough
to be quick-sighted — for the jest now
He tax'd me with eloping with his Sister —
Well we had now best join the
Company .   &c —

R. So! who now can ever have faith in Women

d-d deceitful wanton — why did she not fairly
tell me that she was weary of my Addresses — that
woman Like — her mind was changed — and another Fool
succeeded —

Enter Lady S.

[Lady S.]   Come Clerimont — who[sic] do you leave us — think of
my losing this Hand — (she has no Art) — five
mate —

[Cler.]   Deceitful wanton! —

[Lady S.]   spadille —

[Cler.]   O Yes ma'am–twas very hard —

[Lady S.]   But you seem disturbed — and where are Maria
and Sr Benjamin — I vow I shall be jealous of
Sr Benjamin —

[Cler.]   I dare swear they are together very happy — but
Lady Sneerwell — you may perhaps of Late have perceived
that I am discontended[sic] with Maria — I ask you
to tell me sincerly — have you ever perceived
it —

[Lady S.]   I wish you woud excuse me —

[Cler.]   Nay you promised me — I know you hate deceit —

and deceitful wanton [23] — why did she not fairly
tell me that she was weary of my Address — that
woman like — her mind was changed & another fool
succeeded — — — Enter Lady — S.
come Clerimont — who do you leave us — think of
my losing this Hand — (she has no Art) — five
mate —

Deceitful wanton! —
spadille —
O yes ma'am — two, very hard —
But you seem disturbed — & where are Maria
& S⁰ Benjamin — — — — I vow, I shall be jealous of
S⁰ Benjamin —

C. I dare swear they are together very happy — but
Lady Sneerwell — you may perhaps of late have perceived
that I am discontented with Maria — I ask you
to tell me sincerely — have you ever perceived
it —
I wish you would excuse me —
Nay you promised me — I know you hate de-
-ceit — —

⟨Doctors Fees weighing
weigh their Arguments at Election
Cut a Sheep in two
Change guineas for [illegible] what do ye call em
Paid by Landlord almost not weigh
John can't read Date — but[?] Child must go without
The Natural gravitation of the effects of corruption
Contempt will be begot towards the kings Image when
we are used to see him scalped. — or
an eye knock'd out
The Gold to be called in by proclamation and a general
tax to restore its value — for then twould be e-
qual and laid on ~~such~~. Plate best —
bribed us for light Guineas and sold us for heavy
ones
La[w]yers first handling Scales. or Physicians

Blac. the Kings image in Reverence. when every Shop keeper
comes with his Shears and takes him by the Nose.
       I now see the reason Clerimonts delays to fix the Day
     Her Name is Lady Isabella Air castle
   Isabella Air castle come forth!
       Sr C. I know her intamately. —
Harriet promises Lady S. not to let Maria see her — but
hearing her Brothers Voice come out and runs in again⟩

Doctors fees. weighing
..... weigh their Arguments at Election
but a Sheep in two .
Change guineas for .. but what do ye call em
Paid by Land Lord durst not weigh
John can't read Date — 6th ..... ye. without
The Natural gravitation of the effects of corruption.
Contempt will be kept towards of kings Image when
we are used to see his scalped . — or
an eye knock'd out . —
The Gold to be called if by proclamation & a general
tax to restore its value . for then twould be e:
=qual & laid of not Plate best . —
bribed as for eight Guineas & sold as bad being
ones .
Lawyers foot handling Scales . as Physicians
Blue the Kings mozz in reverence . when every Shop keeper
... with his Shears & takes him by the Nose .
I now see the reason Harriett delays to fix the Day
Her Name is Lady Isabella Aircastle .
Isabella Aircastle come forth .
X .... S.O. I know her intimately . —
Harriet promises Lady I. not to let Maria see her — but
hearing her Brothers Voice come out & more again

65

⟨And learn from Emma's Eyes —

at end
we could or we would or
such ambiguous givings out — this swear —

to sin in her own Defence —

when once she suspects what I would be at — she grows
so familiar that she'd be disapointed if I didn't make the
Attempt. —

The Critick — when He gets out of his Carriage should
always recollect that his Footman from behind is gone
up to judge as well as himself — ⟩

at End

we could or we would or
such ambiguous givings out — this devour —

to sin in her own Defence —

when once she suspects what I would be at — she grows
so familiar that she'd be disapointed if I did n't make the
Attempt. —

X
The Critick — when he gets out of his Carriage should
always recollect that his Footman gone behind is gone
up to judge as well as himself —

⟨Dodsley's Grey's Elegy —
we should make allowance for Age —
But if she drinks acid, and hurts[?], her fat sides every morning
behind a coach Horse to be sure she is to be pitied —
goes abroad to take care of her Character —

— The School for Scandal —

go you scandalous Toad —

Mrs P. your servant Sr Benjamin — the world says scandalous
things of you — but there is no minding what the
world says — why it was but just now I heard
that miss air castle had gon[e] off with — Captn
Saunter —

Maria — wasn't that the miss melville that they ta[l]kd
no Sir — Puppies might have talk'd —
                                        Babble Bore —
The Letter I forgot to loose —
disapointed in marriage — she expects —
The Character of a Prude is hurt by a scandalous Tale as the strongest
constitutions are most hurt by a Fever — but there is a kind of sickly —
Reputation — that holds up a long-time —
— in the Dark —
She is a sort of valedudinaring — in Reputation being conscious —
how delicate the [illegible] Character is — she preserves it with great attention
He has taken your Brother's Name — she indited the Letter —
to do wrong to become more cautious — loose her Vertue to preserve
        her Reputation
I have received an anonymous Letter — ⟩

Dodsley's, Gray's Elegy — —
we should make allowance for Age —
But if she drinks and, & paints, her foll rides every mouerning
behind a coal Heaver to say, she is to be pitied —
— goes abroad to take care of her Character —

— The School for Scandal —

Go you scandalous Toad —

Sir P. your Servant Sir Benjamin — the world says scandalous
things of you — but there is no minding what the
world says — why it was but just now I heard
that miss verjuice had you off with Cat —
Launter — —

Maria — wasn't that the miss melville that they talk'd
no Sir — Puppies might have talk'd —
Rabble Rose —

The Letter I forgot to loose — —

disapointed in marriage — she expects —

The Character of a Prude is hurt by a scandalous Tale as the strongest
constitution are most hurt by a Fever — but there is a kind of sickly
Reputation — that spoils up a long time — —
— in the Dark —

She is a sorte of valedictionaria — her Reputation being cautious —
how delicate the her Character — she preserves it will great attention

She has taken your Brother's Name —   she indite the Letter —
to do wrong to become more cautious. loose her Virtue to preserve her Reputation —

I have received an anonymous Letter — —

SIR PETER TEAZLE

SIR PETER TEAZLE

Sr Rowland Harpur —
~~Joseph~~ — Plausible
Capt. Harry   Brothers and his ~~brothers~~ Nephews
Freeman —
~~Old~~ Sir Peter Teezle   left off Trade —

~~Mrs~~ Lady Teezle —
Maria —

Mischief between Lady Teezle and Sir Peter

Sⁱʳ Rowland Harper –
Joseph – Plausible
Capt. Harry   Brothers & his Neighbours –
        Freeman –
Sⁱʳ Rob͡t. Teezle –   Left off Trade –

        Lady Teezle
        Maria –

        Mischief between Lady Teazle & Sir Peter –

Act 1st Scene 1st

— Old Teezle alone —

In — forty three — I married my first wive — the wedding was —
at the end of the year — aye — twas in December — yet before
anno Dom — forty five — I repented — a month before
we swore we preferr'd each other before
the world — perhaps we spoke truth — but when
we came to promise to love each other till Death —
There I am sure we lied — well — Fortune ow'd — me
a good Turn — in forty eight she died — ah — silly Solomon
in fifty two I find thee married again — here too is
a catalogue of ills — Thomas born — feb. 12th — Jane
born — Jan. 64th — and they go on to the number of five —
however by death I stand church'd but by one — well
margery rest her soul — was a quiet Creature — and
when she was gone I felt awkward at first — and
being — sensible that wishes avail'd — nothing — I after wish'd
for her Return — for ten years now I kept my senses — and
liv'd single — O Blockhead — dolt Solomon — winthin [sic] this twelvemonth
thou art married again — married to a woman ~~twenty~~ —
thirty years younger than thy self — a fashionable woman
[~~illegible words~~] yet I took her with caution — she
had been educated in the country — but now she
has more extravagance than — the Daughter of an
Earl — more levity than a Countess — what a Defect
it is in our Laws — that a man who has

- Old Teazle alone -

In - forty three — I married my first wife .. the wedding was - at the end of the year - aye - twas in December - yet before and Dora - forty five I repented - a month before we ... we ... each other before the world - perhaps we spoke ... truth - but when we came to promise to love each other till Death There I am sure we lied - well - Fortune ow'd me a good Turn - in forty eight she died - ah silly Solomon in fifty two I find thee married again -- here too is a catalogue of ills - Thomas born - Feb. 12 - Jane born - Jan. 6 - & they go on to the number of five - however by ... I stand ... but by one - - well mongery rest her soul - was a quiet creature ... and when she was gone I ... at first - and being sensible that wishes avail'd nothing - I after wish'd for her Return - for ten years now I kept my ... - & liv'd single - O Blockhead - dolt Solomon - within this twelvemonth there art married again married to a woman ... thirty years younger than thy self - a fashionable woman ... yet I took her with caution - She had been educated in the country - but now she has more extravagance than - the Daughter of an Earl - more levity than a Countess - what a Defect it is in our Laws - that a man who has

been once branded in the Forehead — should be
hang'd for the second Offence —

Enter — Jarvis —

Who's there — well Jarvis — ?

Jerv.	Sir ~~they~~ There are a number of my Mistress's Trades[men] without very clamorous for their money —
Teazle	Are those their Bills in your Hand?
Jarv.	something about a twentieth Part — Sir —
Teaz.	What! — have you expend[ed] the hundred — Pounds I gave you for [her] use
Jerv.	Long ago Sir — as you may Judge by some of the Items.
~~Teaz.~~	— Paid the Coachmaker for — lowering the Front seat of the Coach! —
Teaz.	What the Deuce — was [the] matter with the seat —
Jerv.	O lord it was too low for [her] by a Foot when she was dress'd — so that it must have been so — or have had — a tilt at Top like a Hat-Case on a Travelling Trunk —
Teaz.	Well Sir —
[Jerv.]	Item paid her two Footmen half a year's wages — 50£ —
Teaz.	Sdeath — and fury — does — she give her Footmen 100 [a] Year —
Jerv.	Yes Sir and I think that indeed she has — rather made a good Bargain — for they find their own Bags and Boukets —

been once branded in the Forehead — should be hang'd for the second Offence —

Enter — Jarvis —

Who's there — well Jarvis — ?

Jar: — Sir ~~there~~ There are a number of my Mistress's Trades without any clamours for their money — —

Tea: Are those their Bills in your hand ?

Jar: Something about a twentieth Part — Sir.

Tea: What! — have you spend the hundred Pounds I gave you for them

Jar: Long ago Sir — as you may Judge by some of the Items.

~~Tea~~ — — Paid the landlady for — lowering the Front seat of the Coach ? —

Tea: What the Deuce — was matter with the seat —

Jar: Stand it was too low for her by a Foot — when she was dress'd — if that it would having been so — or have had — a tell of Toft a Hot-house on a Travelly Tomb —

Tea: well Sir —

Item, paid her two Footmen half a years wages — £40

Tea: S'death & furry — does she give her Foot 100 year —

Jar: yes Sir & I think that indeed she has rather much in good Bargain — for they find their own Bags & Pockets

//you will not allow me to a regular income
to pay my serv//

Teaz.   Bags — and Boukets for Footmen — Halters and Bastinados —
            well Sir go on —

[Jerv.]   Paid for my Lady's own Nosegays — 50£ —

[Teaz.]   Fifty — Pounds for Flowers *//might turn the Pantheon into a*
                    GreenHouse// — zounds — you migh[t]
            give a Fete Champetre at Xmas —

Lad T.   Lard — Sr Peter — I wonder you should — grudge one the
            most innocent Articles — in Dress — and for the expence — Flowers —
            cannot be cheaper in winter — you should — find fault
            with the Climate and not with me — I'm sure I wish
            with all my Heart — that it was spring all the year
            round — and that Flowers *//Roses//* grew under our *//one's//* Feet — !

Sr P.   Nay but madam — ~~tell me can you find any satisfaction in wearing them~~
                    and then you would not wear them —
            but try some thirsty [?] snow Balls
            and Icicles — but tell me madam — can you
            find any satisfaction in wearing them — when
            you might Refle[c]t thus — that one [of] the Rose Buds
            might have furnish'd a poor Family with
            a Dinner —

Lad T.   Upon my word Sir Peter — begging your Pardon
            that is a very absurd way — of [~~illegible~~] arguing —
            by that rule why do you — indulge — in the
            least superfluit[y] — I dare swear — a Beggar
            might — dine tolerably on your great-Coat —
            or Sup off your laced waistcoat — nay
            I dare swear He wouldn't eat your
            gold headed Cane in a week — nay
            if you would require nothing but
            Necessaries you should give the first
            ~~Post~~ poor man the [sic] wants his wig —
            and walk the streets in your Night-cap
            which you know well [?] becomes him so

you will not allow me to a regular

Sir Peter ... ... fortune — Slibber ... — well Sir go on —

Besides you may ... Nosegays 50 th ... Fifty Pounds for Flowers — ... you might ... a fete Champetre at Xmas —

Lady T. Lard — Sir Peter — I wonder you should grudge me the most innocent Articles — in Dress — & for the expence. flowers cannot be cheaper in winter — you should find fault with the Climate & not with me — I'm sure I wish with all my Heart — that it was Spring all the year round — & that Flowers grew under our Feet —

Sir P. Nay but madam — ... you would not wear them — ... but try ... — but tell me madam — can you find any satisfaction in wearing them — when you might reflect that one ... might have furnish'd a poor Family with a Dinner —

Lady T. Upon my word Sir Peter — begging your Pardon that is a very absurd way — of arguing — by that rule why do you indulge in the least superfluity — I have heard — a Person might — dine tolerably on your great. knob or Sirloin of your laced waist ... — ... I dare swear the ... it would it eat your gold headed Cane in a week — ...

79

	much —
[Sir P.]	well go on to the Articles —
[Jerv.]	Fruit — for — my Lady's Monkey — 5 sh per week —
[Sir P.]	five — for the monkey — why 'tis a Des[s]ert for an Alderman
[Lady T.]	Why — Sr Peter would you starve the poor Animal? I dare swear He lives as reasonably as other Monkeys do —
[Sir P.]	Well well go on —
[Jerv.]	China — for D[itt]o —
[Sir P.]	Hey — what does He eat out of China —
[Jerv.]	Repairing china — that He breaks — 5 —
[Lady T.]	And I am sure no monkey breaks less —
[Jerv.]	Paid Mr. Warren for Perfumes — milk of Roses — 30£
[Lady T.]	Very Reasonable —
[Sir P.]	Sdeath Madam — if ~~these~~ you had [been] bred to these — expences — I should not be so much amazed — but I took — you madam an honest country Squires Daughter
[Lady T.]	O Filthy — don't — name it — well Heav'n forgive my mother but I do beleive my Father must have been a man of Quality —
[Sir P.]	— yes madam — when First I saw you you were drest — a pretty — figured Linen — with a bunch — of ~~house~~ Keys by your Side

80

much ─

       will go on to the Articles ─

First ─ for my Lady's Monkey ─ at £ per week ─
five ─ for the monkey ─ why 'tis a Dear foo an Alderm—
Why Sir Peter would you starve the poor innocent ?
I dove breed the livee as reasonably as other
Monkeys do ─

Well well go on ─

China ─ to Do ─

Hey ─ what does the eat out of China ─
Repairing china ─ that the breaks ─ 5 ─
And I am sure no monkey breaks left ─

Paid Mr. Warren for Perfumes ─ milk of Roses ─ 30
Very Reasonable ─

Sheath Madam ─ if you had bred to
there ─ expences ─ I should not bee so much
amazed ─ ─ but I took ─you madam
an honest country Squire's Daughter ─

O Filthy ─ dont ─ name it ─ well heav'n
forgive my mother, but I do believe my
Father must have been a man of Quality
─ Yes madam ─ when First I saw you you
wore duoff ─ a Pretty ─ figured linen ─ with
a bunch of keys by your side

— your occupation madam — to superintend
the Poultry — your accomplishment — a complete
Knowledge of the Family — receipt Book —
there you sat ma'am — in Room hung round
with Fruit in worsted of your own
working — your accomplishments ma'am
to play country Dances //a game of Picquet with the Curate// — on an
    old Spinet
to your //to play him to sleep after a Foxchase// — Father while he went
    to Sleep —
or to read Tillots[on's] sermons — to your Aunt Deborah —
These madam were your Recreations —
and these were the Accomplishments that cap-
tivated me — //and in Xmas to play at cross Questions
or hunt the Slipper — //

[Lady T.]   O shocking —

[Sir P.]   Now forswooth [sic] — you must have two
footmen to your chair — and a pair of coach
Dogs in a Phaeton — you forget when you
used — to ride double — behind the Butler —
on a dock'd bay Coach-Horse —

[Lady T.]   Barbarous

[Sir P.]   Now you must have a French — Hair Dresser —
Feathers — do you think you do not look
as well when you had your hair
comb'd smooth over a Roler —
~~With Sr Peter~~ Then you could be content to sit with
me or walk — by the side of the Ha!ha! —

[Lady T.]   True I did — and when you ask'd me
if I could love — an old Fellow

your occupation weeding to superintend
the Poultry — your accomplishment — a complete
Knowledge of the Family — receipt Book —
there you set men in those being used
with Fruit in worsted of your own
working — your accomplishment   a game of Piquet will the lovearte
to keep your two Voices   on held Skeines
to your   to play give to dress after a Foxchase
or read Filots Preview — to your Aunt Jehovah —
These weedon were your Recreations —
& these were the Accomplishment that cap-
tivated me — a super to fly at cross Questive
& shooting —   or hunt at Slippers —
Now forthwith — you will have two
footmen to your chair — & a pair of each
Days in a Phaeton — you bought when you
used — to ride double — behind the Brother
on a docked bay coach Horse —
Now Purchasing you must have a French & Hair dresser
& festons — do you think you do not look
as well when you had your Hair
combed smooth over a Rolar —
you could be content to sit with
me or walk by the side of the   be —
I were I did — & when you ate'd me
if I could have an ld Villows

	who would deny — me nothing — I simpered I said — till Death — Did you think age was catching
[Sir P.]	Why did you say so —
[Lady T.]	Shall I tell you the Truth —
[Sir P.]	If it is not two [sic] great a Favour —
[Lady T.]	Why then the Truth is I was heartily tired of all those agreeable Recreations you have so well remember'd — ~~and was de~~ and having a spirit to spend and enjoy a Fortune I was de- termined to marry the first Fool I could meet with —
[Sir P.]	Why fix //So pray what induced you to fix on me O your youth and personal accomplishment to be sure// on me
[Lady T.]	To say truth your Age — would have been an insu~~rmount~~perable objection — But as I prudently consider'd that as a maid I was then so anxious to be wife — I might when a wife wish as much to be a widow ~~so I consider'd that you made me a wife~~ ~~for which I am~~
[Sir P.]	if I were to die what would you do
[Lady T.]	countermand my new Brocade —
[Sir P.]	You might have [been] maid still but for me —
[Lady T.]	Well you made me a Wife — for which I am much obliged to you and if you have a mind to make me more grateful still make me

who would deny me nothing — I smiled
I said to[?] ... did you think age
was ...

Why did you say so —

Shall I tell you the Truth —

If it is not too great a Favour —

Why then the Truth is I was frightened
of all those agreeable Recollections you have
so well remember'd — ... de a having
a spirit to spend & enjoy a fortune I was de-
-termined to marry the first Fool I could
meet with —

Why fix so long on me? your youth & personal accomplishments ...
So say youth your Age would have
been an insuperable objection — But, as
I prudently consider'd that as a maid I was
then so anxious to be wife — I might we
a wife brisk as ready to be a widow
and consider'd that you ... ... a wife
for which I am if I were to die what would
you do countermand my new Promise —
you might have maid still but for
me —

Well you made me a Wife — for
which I am much obliged to you &
if you have a mind to oblige
me more grateful still more me

a widow —

[Sir P.]   Soh! what did you marry me for — ?

[Lady T.]   Good — Heav'n what a Question — after
               you have — answer'd — it yourself — why
               to ride in a Viz a viz — to be servd in-
               stead of the Pillion behind the Butler —
               and to change those rural ~~elegant~~ Diversion you
               have — so elegantly praised — for those
               more to my Taste which you rail at.

[Sir P.]   Then you never had a Desire to please me
               or add to my Happiness —

[Lady T.]   Seriously I never thought about you — did you
               imagine that age was catching — and
               I think you have been overpay'd — for all you
               could bestow on me — Here am I surrounded
               by half a hundred Lovers — not one — of whom
               but by [sic] a single smile by a thousand such
               Baubles as you grudge me —

[Sir P.]   But you continue to deny me — tho tis hard a
               Husband should furnish his Wife with means
               to make a conquest —

[Lady T.]   I can answer if you indulge me [sic] Vanity —

[Sir P.]   Then you wish me dead —

[Lady T.]   You know I do not — for you have made no
               settlement on me —

[Sir P.]   Soh The Devil of it is — I indulged so much at first

86

a widow ——————————————————

To but what did you marry me for?
Good — Heaven what a Question — after
you have — interval'd — it yourself — ally
to ride in a Vis-a-vis. to be rivel in
instead of the Pillion behind the Butler —
& to change those elegant Diversion you
were — so elegantly praised — for those
more to my taste which you rail at —

Then you never had a Desire to please me
or held to my Happiness —

Sincerely I never thought about you — did you
imagine that age was catching ———— and
I think you have been overpay'd — for all you
call bestows on me ——— Have am I surrounded
by half a hundred Lovers — not one of whom
but by a single smile by a such
Baubles as you grudge me — ———

But you continue to deny me — the tie head a
Husband should furnish his wife with means
to make a conquest —

I am content if you indulge me Vanity —— —

Then you wish me dead —

You know I do not — for you have made no
settlement on me — —— —

And the Devil of it is — I indulged so much at first

that People will now say tis Jealousy
should I confine her — I humour'd her at
first and had a Delight in seeing her dress'd
out — little imagining in what thriving soil
I was cultivating Fopery and Dissipation —
Then Madam to ~~pass over~~ say no more of your expences
I do extremely dislike the Company you keep —

[Lady T.]   My dear Sr Peter you should certainly not find Fault
when the Remedy is in your Power — you have nothing
to do but to keep out of our Society — but pray Sir
what are your objections to my company! They are
all of them People of Fortune and Character —
// The company is very good when you do not spoil it//

[Sir P.]   The greatest objection in Nature — what [sic] they are a
people //yet they are// — of so nice a
Reputation //and as you observe so tenacious in that Point that// that
they don't chuse any body should have a character but themselves

[Lady T.]   Lord — now — how ill nature[d] you are to make no
allowance for a turn for Raillery
//tenacious of Reputation//

[Sir P.]   no madam — the scandal woud — utterers — of lies —
knowing them — coiners of [illegible], and clippers
of Reputation — ~~the~~ in the Person w[h]o utters
a Tale of scandal knowing — it be forged —
deserves Pillory more than for a Bank Note —
only they cannot Pass the Bill — without
sometimes their Name on the Back of
a Lie — hurts the credit — you say —
the Person has no Right to come on

that People will now say two guineas
should I confine her — I humour'd her at
first & had a Delight in seeing her dress'd
out — little imagining in what thriving soil
I was then cultivating Foppery & Extravagance —

Then Madam to your more of
I do extremely dislike the company you keep —
My dear Sr Peter you should certainly not find Fault
when the Remedy is in your Power — you have nothing
to do but to keep out of our society — but pray Sir
what are your objections to my company? they are
all of them People of Fortune & Character —
The company is one when you do not find
The greatest objection in Nature — what they are a
People — of so nice a Reputation that they don't chuse
that any body should have a character but themselves.
— And now how ill nature you are to make no
allowance for a turn for Raillery —
no reason — the scandal would utters of both
the knowing them — esing of scandal, a dippens
of Reputation — the in the Person are others
a Joke of scandal knowing — it be forged —
deserves Pillory more than for a Banker Note —
only they can't Pass the Bill, without
writing their Name on the Back of
a Lie — hurts the credit — you say —
the Person has no Right to come on

89

you because you didn't invent it but you should
know that if the Drawer of the Lie is out —
the way — the injured Party has a Right to come
on any of the Indorsers —

what have you to do with Taste — you had no Taste —
when I married —

[Lady T.]   Tis very — true indeed — I should not pretend to
Taste after having married you —

[Sir P.]   I am — but middle-aged —

[Lady T.]   There's the misfortune — put yourself on or back twenty years and
[it] will do — and either way I should like you the better.
Yes Sir, and then your behaviour too was different you
could dress — and smile and bow — fly to fetch — me anything I wanted —
then you prais'd everything I did or said — fatigue[d] your
stiff Face with an eternal smile grin — and affect //disgracing your
        gravity// — a youthful tread —
Because you are old enough to be my Father you exert the severity of one —
mufling — your harsh Tones — with a lovers whisper — that was why
mother said you were the smartest old batchelor she ever saw —
Billedoux — engross'[d] on Buckram — !!!!!!

//and made stiff — 'Tis false the
verses were as good as ever were made and the Rhymes true//
//nay you committed Poetry
and to do justice — to a Song you made you attempted
once to sing it yourself — //

[Sir P.]   What ungenerous Banter [~~illegible words~~] —

[Lady T.]   A woman let her take my advice — and never marry —
an old Batchelor — he must be so either because He
could find nothing to Love in women or because
no woman could find any thing to love in him —

— You prize and deify 'till you leave us nothing — to bestow —
and then you hold cheap — what wonder the[n] that we look
out for that incense from others —
If you would have us prize our charms — don't seem to
hold them cheap — lest we make them so and think the
favour not worth denying to any one that asks it — and
appears to prize us more — the[y] deserve a Ladys Favours
who set most value on their charms —

90

you because you did n't in week but you should
know that if the ?nour? of the die is out
the way — the injured Party has a right to come
on any of the Endor?——

see nt
2d Si. 1.
8o Editn
P. 41

what have you to do with Taste — — you had no taste
when I married —
'Tis very true indeed — I should not pretend to
Taste after having married you —
I am — but middle-aged.
There's the misfortune — put yourself on or back twenty years I
will do — & either way I should like you the better.
You sir and then your behaviour too was different, you
would dress & smile & bow — fly to fetch me any thing I wanted
they you prais'd everything I did or said — fatigue your
stiff Face with an eternal smile given — & offer ?it? a ?your? ?trea??
because you are old you throught be my flatter you used to severity often one
made stiff — ?may? you commit? ?Poplin? & took ?iyptic? for a ?tough? of made ?you? ?oftentee
Tis false the humbling — your heart fails — with a lower whisper — that was very
verses were ever I te ?gon? it yourself — ?as good as? ?another? face you were the smartest old batcheler she ever saw
too une ind? Villedoux engrass'or Buckvaw — !!!!!!!
the Abequartere?

What ungenerous ?Bruter? ise ??? — — — — —
A woman let her take my advice — never marry —
an old Batchelor — he must be so either because he
could find nothing to love in women or because
a woman could find any thing to love in him — — —

you praise & deify 'till you leave us nothing to bestow —
& then you hold cheap — what wonder then that we look
out for that incense from others —
If you would have us prize our charms — don't seem to
hold them cheap — led me ?value them? so I ?think? the
favour not worth desiring to any one that asks it &
appear to prize us more — The clogene a ?let? of favours
who set most value on their charms —

⟨If you mortify us why should [we] reserve our
Favour[s] for those who are insensible of them.⟩

if you mortify us why should reserve our
Favour for those who are incredible of them. —

⟨universal Good Character —
I don't like every-body's speaking well of him
keep a wench —
At his Age I kept too [sic]

every body speaks well of him — I'm sorry
to hear it — for then he must have paid more
homage to vice than merit —
He has too Good — a character to be an honest Fellow⟩

uncommon good Character —

I don't like every-body's speaking well of him
— keep a — —

At his Age I thought too

every body speaks well of him — I'm sorry
to hear it — for then he must be been paid more
honour to me than merit.

He has too good-character to be an honest fellow.

⟨tho' to do him justice He has
some acquired vices of which however
He has too vain —

Scene 1st

The Poor Unkle — and young Surface —
This is the bad Effect of a good Character

has often Vice in his mouth — and never
in his heart — affects to be profligate and solicits
an ill name — does good by stealth and is vain //osten[ta]tious//
only of Vices —

in the midst — of all this vulgartity [sic]
A vulgar Fellow — tho' to do him [justice] He has some coar[s]e [?]
fashionable Vices of which however he is too vain — which
would become him well enough only He is too vain of them
Aye youre one pertains to him (or her) and beleive He gauges⟩

96

tho' to do him justice He has
some acquired vices of which however
He has too vain ~

The poor Clerkule - & young Surface ..

This is one bad Effect of a good Character.

Nay often Vice in his mouth - & never
in his heart - affects to be profligate & solicits
an ill name .. - does good by stealth & is vain only of Vices
ostentious

in the midst - of all their ingenuity
A vulgar Fellow - tho' to do him He has some acquired
fashionable Vices of which however he is too vain - which
would become him well enough only he is too vain of them

"Aye youve are partner to him forbear [& believe He gay

97

Scene

— Young Pliant's — Room —

I wonder her Ladyship is not here she promised me to call this
morning — I have a hard Game to Play here to pursue my
Designs on Maria — I have brought myself into a Scrape with
the mother in Law — However I think we have taken care
to ruin my Brother's character beyond ~~the~~ his Power to
retreive it with my unkle should He arrive tomorrow.
Frank has not an ill Qu[a]lity in his Nature — yet a Neglect
of Forms and of the opinion of the World has hurt him
in the Estimation of all his graver Friends — I have
profited by his Errors — practiced to gain a Character —
which now serves me [as] a mask to lie under — Frank —
see who it is thro' the window
now draw the screen —

Enter Lady Teazle —

L.	What musing — or thinking of me —
Y.Pl.	I was thinking unkindly of you — do you know now that you must be so kind to repay me for this Delay — or I must be coax'd into good Humour —
L.T.	Nay in Faith — you should pity me — the old Curmudgeon of late is grown so jealous that I dare scarce go out — 'till I know He is secure for some time —
Y.P.	I am afraid the Insinuations we have had spread for Frank — have operated too strongly on him we meant — only to divert his Suspicions to a wrong object —
L.T.	O Hang him — I have told him Plainly that if He continues to be so suspicious I'll leave him

98

Scene –

– Young Pliant's Room –

I wonder Lady Stile is not here she promised me to call this
morning – I have a hard game to play here to pursue my
Designs in Mania – I have brought myself into a Scrape with
the Mother in Law – however I thing we ceased taken care
to ruine my Brother's character beyond the his Power to
retrieve it with my uncle should He arrive tomorrow.
Frailty has not an ill Quality in his Nature – a Neglect
of forms do the opinion of the World yet hurt him
in the Estimation of all his graver – however I have
profited by his Errors – forced to give a Character –
which now teeries you a mesh to his under – Frank –
see who it is thro' the window
now draw the screen –   Enter Lady Teazle –

L.– What musing – or thinking of me –

Y.P.– I was thinking unkindly of you – do you know now that
you must bee so kind to repay me for this Delay or
I must be coaxed into good Humour –

L.T.– Nay in faith an you should fretty and – was old
Curmudgeon, of late is grown so jealous that I dare scare
you not – till I know he is secure for some
time –

Y.P.– I am afraid the Insinuations we have had spread
for Frank have operated too strongly on him
me meant only to divert his Suspicions to a
wrong object –, – – – –

L.T.– O Hang him – I have told him Plainly that if he
continues to be so suspicious I'll leave him

entirely and make him allow me a seperate
Maintenance —

Y.P.   But my charmer if ever that should be the case
you see before you the man who will ever be attach'd
to you — but you must never let matters come
to extremities — you can never be reveng'd so well
be [sic] leaving him as by living with him — and let my
//For I can plague his life out// sincere Affection make amends for his
      Brutality —

L.T.   — But how shall [I] be sure now that you are sincere —
I have sometimes suspected that you loved my
Neice —

Y.P.   O hang her a puling Idiot — without sense or spirit —

[L.T.]   But what Proofs have I of your Love to me — for I
have still so much of my Country Prejudices
left — that If ever I do a foolish — Thing
(and I [sic] that I can't Promise) it shall be for a Man who
would risk everything for me alone —
How shall [I] be sure you love me —

Y.P.   I have dream'd of you every Night for this week Past —

L.T.   O Fie Thats a sign you have — slept every Night for this week
For my Part I would not give a Pin for [a] Love[r] —
who could not wake for a month in Absence —

[Y.P.]   I have written — Verses on you out of number —

[L.T.]   I never saw any —

[Y.P.]   No — they did not pleas[e] me me and so I tore —

[L.T.]   Then it seems you wrote them only to divert yourself.

100

intirely & make him allow me a seperate
Maintenance —

Y.P. But my dear—s if ever that should be the case
you see before you the One who will ever be attent
to you — but you must never let matters come
to extremities — you can never be reveng'd so well
be leaving him as by living with him — & let my
sincere Affection make amends for his Pretolility —

J.S. But you shall be sure now—that you are since—
I having sometimes suspected that you loved my
Neice —

Y.P. I love her—a feeling Ideal — without sense or spirit —
But what Proofs have I of your love to me — for I
have still so much of my country Prejudices
left — that If ever I do a foolish — I wish
(as I th—k I can't promise) it shall be for a Man who
would wish everything for me alone —
then shall be sure you love me —

Y.P. I dream'd of you every Night for this week Past —

J.S. Oh. That's a light you have—slept every Night for this week
for my Part I would not give a Pin for love —
who could not wake for a month in Absence —
I have written Verses on you out of number —

I never saw any —

No they did not please me so I tore —
You it seems you wrote them only believe yourself.

Y.P.	Am I doom'd for ever to sigh in vain —
[L.T.]	I don't know — if I were — convinced —
[Y.P.]	Then let me on my Knees —
[L.T.]	Nay nay I will have no Raptures either — //tho I don't fancy your overdoing//
	This much — I can tell you that if [I] am to be seduced
	to do wrong — I am not to be taken by Storm
	nor Storm — but a deliberate capitulation —
	and that only where my reason or my Head
	is convinced —
[Y.P.]	Then to say it [at] once the world gives itself Libertys —
[L.T.]	Nay I am sure without cause for I am as yet un-
	conscious of any ill tho' I know not what I may
	be forced to —
[Y.P.]	The Fact is my dear Lady Teaze — that your extreme Innocence
	is the very cause of your Danger — it is the integrity
	of your Heart which makes you run into a
	Thousand Imprudences — which a litt[le] consciousness —
	of Error whould [sic] make you guard against — now
	in that case you can't conceive how much — more
	circumspect you would be —
[L.T.]	Do you think so —
[Y.P.]	most certainly in short — your character — is like
	a person — in a Pl[ethora] — absolutely — dying of too
	much Health
[L.T.]	So then — you [would] have me sin in my own
	Defence — and part with my Virtue to Preserve my
	Reputation —

y. P. do I doom'd for ever to repin vain
I don't know — if I were convinced —
Then let rely on my knowing
2 Nay very well I will have no Reptens either —
This much — I can tell you that if an to be reduced
to do wrong — I am not to be taken by Storm
nor Storm — but a deliberate capitulation —
and that only where my reason or my Head
is convinced —

Then to say it one the world gives itself Liberty —
Nay I am sure without cause for I am as yet on —
consious of any ill — tho' I know not what I may
be forced to —

The Fact is my dear Lady Teare — that your knowing
is the very cause of your Danger — it is the integrity
of your Head which makes you run into a
Thousand Imprudence — which a less conscience
of Error — would make you guard against — were
in that case you can't conceive how much — more
circumspect you would be —

Do you think so —
most certainly in short — your character — is like
a person — in a R — absolutely — dying of too
much Health

So then — you have me laid in my own
Defence — I port with my Virtue to preserve my
Reputation —

[Y.P.]	Exactly so upon my credit Ma'am —
[L.T.]	Well this is the newest Receipt — for avoiding ~~Character~~ Scandal —
[Y.P.]	Beleive me madam — more Ladies save their credit by it than their Innocense — Prudence is the Daughter of experience — experience must be paid for — //I want to convince your understanding for Heaven forbid I should want you to do anything you thought wrong//
[L.T.]	Upon my — word — you are an acute Reason[er] — and I dare swear — in your own [cause] you say you are willing to furnish me with Prudence — so I presume if one finds one self relapsing into levity — one has nothing for it but a new intrigue —

Enter Serv — whispers —

[Y.P.]	Death and Fury — Here's Sir Peter coming up Stairs —
[L.T.]	O mercy — what will become of me —
[Y.P.]	Have haste fly — Hes just Here —

(She runs behind the Screen —)

Enter Sr Peter —

P.	Soh! — Sir Peter — I am rejoiced beyond measure to see you — P[s]haw — I [~~illegible~~] have been pouring here over a Book till I am nearly — blind — (*flings it away*)
[Sir P.]	Ah — you are a studious young man — what's — you are study[ing] — but I am come to speak with you on some particular Business — let us be alone —

Equally so when any credit it thrown —
Well this is the newest Receipt for avoiding ~~Character~~
Scandal —
Believe me madam — nore [...] [...] their credit ??
if than their Inocence — Prudence is the Daughter of experience
& experience must be paid for —

Upon my — word — you I [...] to convince your understanding
for Heaven forbid I should want you to do
are [...] Reason — and anything you thought wrong —
I have [...] in your own [...] [...] you are
willing to furnish me with Prudence — so I [...]
if one finds one self [...] in [...] — one has
nothing for it but a new intervens ——

Enter Lady [...] whispers —

Death & Fury — Here's Sir Peter coming up Stairs —

[H] Oons — what will become of me —
Here here step —
Here just [...]

(He runs behind the Screen —)

Enter Sr. Peter —

[P] Joh!— Sir Peter — I am rejoiced beyond measure to see you —
Phaw — I ~~have~~ have been poring here over
a Book till I am nearly — blind — — (flings it away)
Ah — you are a studious young man — what's —
you are study — — but I am come to speak
with you on some particular Business —
let me be alone —

—P	Fury — get about your Business —
Sr P.	Now then we are alone — I must open my mind to you — in short my dear Friend Lady Teazle's Conduct — makes me very miserable — it isn't her Expence — but between ourselves I think I have of late perceived in her — //discover'd the Person// an Attachment to another — and from various things I have heard —
[P.]	The Devil I hope not —
[Sir P.]	Alas I fear it is but too true //And what is more I think I have discovered the Person// I know you would sympathize with me
[P.]	Yes beleive — me Sr Peter such a Discovery would give me equal uneasiness with yourself — but who do you suspect — ?
[Sir P.]	Can't you guess —
[P.]	I haven't the most distant Idea —
[Sir P.]	No — yet the thing concerns you — nearly —
[P.]	How Sir — Peter —
[Sir P.]	Nay — what do you think — I meant you — no no no — my Friend I know your Principles too well —
[P.]	I should hope so Sir Peter —
[Sir P.]	But what think you of your Brother?
[P.]	Who Frank impossible — put such Thoughts from you Sr Peter — some ill-designing People have put this into your did [sic] — no no Frank — wouldn't be guilty of such a Thing //So is//

– O prey – get about your Business –

Si P. now then we are alone – I must open my
mind to you – in that my dear Friend Lady
Teazles conduct makes me very miserable –
it is n't her Expence – but between ourselves, I think
I have of late perceived in her an ^discovery the Person^ Attachment
to another – & from various things I have heard –

+ The Devil I hope not –

x Alas I fear it is but too true
And what is more I think I have discovered
^the Person^ would sympathize with me
yes believe me Si Peter such a Discovery would
give me equal uneasiness with yourself –
but who do you suspect —?

can't you guess –

I have n't the most distant Idea –

No – yet the thing concerns you. nearly –
How Si Peter –

Nay – what do you think – I meant you – no
no no – my Friend I know your Principles
too well –

I should hope so Si Peter –

But what think you of your Brother?

Si P] Who Frank insossible – put such Thoughts
from you Si Peter – some Hill-designing
People have put this into your Head –
no no Frank – would the guilty of such a thing

//I should think — tho' there's no knowing People
there is no knowing//

[Sir P.]   Ah! you judge of him but [sic] yourself — but I have
weighty reasons to suspect him —

[P.]   I own I don't think she is capable of wronging you
a little imprudent perhaps but rely on't she has
had [too] much principle to do an essential wrong —

[Sir P.]   Aye but what's her Principle when she is assail'd by
an artful — young-Fellow —

[P.]   Thats very true —

[Sir P.]   And then you [know] the difference of our ages makes it
impossible for her to love me — and if she was
to be frail every body would laugh — at the old
Fool for marrying a Girl —

[P.]   This is true — to be sure //Sr Peter — they would laugh —
yes they would laugh at the old Fellow — //

[Sir P.]   But then again — that a son of ~~Sr~~ my old Friend
Sr Rowlande — should be the Person hurts me
still more — I that have been in a manner been
left your Guardian — to come to my house under
the mask — of Friendship —

[P.]   O 'tis not to be credited — there may to be sure
be such men living but till I am convinced
of it I cannot credit it — however if it
should be the case He is no longer a Brother
of mine — I disclaim kindred — with him —
for the man — who can break thro' the Laws
of hospitality and but in Thought — attempt the
wife of his Friend should be chased from
society as a monster —

//Sr Peter to mention Y. Surfaces match with his Daughter —
— which he is afraid of Lady T's overhearing —
Sr I ~~better~~ Peter I beg you won't mention it —
— I am too much affected to touch on that subject now//

- Ah! you judge of men but yourself — but there is
weighty reasons to suspect him —

I own I don't think she is capable of wronging you
a little imprudent perhaps but rely on't she has
had much principle to do an special wrong —

— Aye but what's her Principle when she is spoil'd by
an artful — young — fellow. —

That's very true —

And then you the difference of our ages makes it
impossible for her to love me — and if she was
to be frail every body would laugh — at the old
Fool for marrying a Girl. . . .

This is true — to be sure — Peter — they would laugh —
yes they would laugh at the old fellow —
But then again — that a son of — my old Friend
S.r Rowland — should be the Person hurt me
still more — I that have been in a manner been
left your Guardian — to come to my house under
the mask — of Friendship. — —

It 'tis not to be credited — there may to be sure
be such men living but till I am convinced
of it I cannot credit it — however if it
should be the case He is no longer a Brother
of mine — I disdain kindred with him —
for the man — who can break thro' the laws
of hospitality & but in thought — attempt the
wife of his Friend should be chased from
society as a monster —

[Sir P.]   Ah! my Friend you are a man of sentiment
             it is edification to hear you — there is nothing so
             noble as fine sentiments — yet my Friend beleive
             me I would do everything in my Power to make her Happy — it was
             but this morning she as good as told me she wish'd me
             dead — yet if I was did [sic] she would — find — that I have been
             attentive to her Interests while living — at the same time too
             she reproach'd me with having settled nothing on her —
             now as I received no Fortune with her — I omitted [illegible]
             thinking to bind her to me by me [sic] Liberality — but as
             we seem to differ in our Ideas of expence — I have
             departed — termined to make — her her own mistress
             in that respect for the Future — Here my Friend
             are deed are two Deeds — one is my will —
             where in you'll find I have troubled you with the
             executorship — and some remembrance —

[P.]   O Sir — Peter —

[Sir P.]   This other is a Deed in trust by which I convey and
             setle five hundred — Pound for Pin money on her
             during my Life —

[P.]   What would you have done with them — Sir — ?

[Sir P.]   I have brought these two for you to witness and execute —

[P.]   Sir — you may depend on it this confidence will meet
             with a grateful return — [I] shall witness them now — by
             Pen and ink — I wish this generosity may not corrupt my Pupil —

                         — *Enter Ser[vant]* —

[Servant]   Sir — your Brother //and stept in next Door// is speaking to a
                   Gentleman
             below and says He'll call on you in a few minutes

Ah: my Friend you are a man of sentiment
it is edification to hear you – there is nothing so
noble as fine sentiments – yet my Friend believe
me I would do everything in my Power to make her Happy – it was
this morning she as good as told me she wish'd me
dead – yet if I was did she would find – that I have been
attentive to her Interests while living – at the same time too
she reproach'd me with having settled nothing on her –
now as I received no Fortune with her – I own I thought Nothing
thinking to bind her to me by my kindness – but as
we seem to differ in our Ideas of expence – I have
determined to make her her own mistress
of in that respect for the Future – I have my Friend
two Deeds – one is my will
wherein you'll find I have troubled you with the
executorship – as some remembrance –
O Sir – Pray –
They other is a Deed in trust by which I convey
settle five hundred Pound for Pin money on her
during my Life – – –
what would you have done with them Sir ?
I have brought them ten for you to witness & execute –
Sir – you may depend on it this confidence I will meet
with a gratiful return – shall witness them now – &c
Pen & ink – I wish this generosity may not corrupt my Pupil –
– Enter Servant –
Sir – your Brother & sister is speaking to a Gentleman
below & say She'll call on you in a few minutes

[P.]	Tell him not within — we have Business —
[Serv.]	Sir I said you were at home —
[P.]	Did you mention who was here —
[Serv.]	I mention'd only Sir Peter — Sir —
[P.]	Well say I beg He'll call another at [sic] Time —
[Sir P.]	stay hold Frank — a Thought [h]as come into my Head — Oblige me I entreat you ~~tax~~ — let your Brother come — and let me conceal myself somewhere then — then tax — him on — the subject we have been speak[ing] off [sic] then his answer may satisfy me at once —
[P.]	O Fie Sir — Peter — would you have me join in so mean a Trick — to trepan my Brother —
[Sir P.]	Nay you are so you are sure he is innocent if so you will do him a service in giving him an opportunity to clear himself — come you mus[t] my heart is set on't — Here I'll — step behind this Screen — hey — the Devil here seems to be one Listner already — I'll swear I saw a Petticoat —
[P.]	Hah! — hah! well this is ridiculous enough! — I'll tell you Sir — Peter — tho' I hold a man of Intrigue to be a most contemptible Character — yet you know it doesn't follow that a man is to be a

Tell him not within — we have Business —
~~This I said~~ you were at home —
Did you mention who was here —
I mention'd only Sir Peter — Sir —
Well say I beg he'll call another at time — —
stay hold — Frank — a thought as come into my
Head — — Oblige me I entreat you — top. let your
Brother come — & let me conceal myself some ode
then — then top — him on — the subject we have
been speak off then — his answer may satisfy me at once.
— O Five Sir — Peter — would you have me join in
so — mean a Trick — to trepan my Brother —
Nay you 'are — so you are sure he is innocent if so
you will do him a service in giving him an
opportunity to clear himself — come your are in
heart it set on't — Here I'll — step behind
this Screen — — hey — the Devil here seems to
be one Listener already — — I'll swear I saw a
Petticoat —
Hah! — hah! well this is ridiculous enough! — I'll tell
you Sir — Peter — tho' I hold a man of Intrigue
to be a most contemptible Character — yet you
know it does not follow that a man is to be a

Joseph — hearkee — tis a little French milleners Prentice
a silly Fool that plagues me — and being afraid
of being seen on your coming she slipt behind —
the screen —

[Sir P.]   O you're a Rogue — but egad she has over-
heard all I have been saying of my wife —

[P.]   O it shall never go any Further you may depend
on it —

[Sir P.]   Then ifaith let her hear it out — for I am
bent upon this and you shall oblige me —

Enter Ser[vant]

[Serv.]   Sir heres your Brother —

[P.]   Well — get in then — I'll take care He
shall hear no harm —
was ever man in such a situation.

— *Enter Frank* —   //or has she found
out that she has
got an old Husband//

So Brother good morrow — to you —

[Frank]   Hey Tom what the Devil have you been at? —
Your Rascal wouldn't let me in at first —
What have you had a Jew or a wench with you?

[P.]   Neither Brother I assure you —

[Frank]   But what made Sir Peter steal off your Servant
told me he was here at first — what
was the old Fool afraid to meet me —

[P.]   Why Brother to say Truth — it was your coming —
that deprived me of his company — and indeed
the subject we have been upon — requires me

Joseph — — mah-ha — tis a little French Millener Prentice
a silly Fool that plagues me — & being afraid
of being seen on your coming she slipt behind
the screen — — —

O youre 've a Rogue — but equal she has over-
= heard all I have been saying of my wife —
O it shall never go any Further you may depend
on it —

Then afaith let her hear it out — for I am
bent upon that & you shall oblige me —
Will — get in there — I'll take care she
shall hear no harm —

nor was man in such a situation.
— Enter Frank — or how she found
out that she peep
got an old Husband.

So Brother good morrow — to you —

Hey Jou what the Devil have you been at ?
your Rascal would'nt let me in at first —
what have you a Jew or a wench with you ?

Neither Brother I assure you — —

But what made Sr. Peter steal off your Servant
told me he was here at first — what
was the old Fool afraid to meet me — — —

Why Brother to say Truth — it was your coming —
that deprived me of his company — and indeed
the subject we have been upon — requires, we

	to talk with you a little seriously —
[Frank]	Hey what's the matter now —
[P.]	Why it seems something in your — conduct has alarm'd his Jealousy — but I hope you are too much a man of Honor ever to have given any cause for such a suspicion —
[Frank]	Ha! ha! well egad this — is — ridiculous enough. so the old Baronet — begins to find — [h]is young wife has a better taste than He thought —
[P.]	Nay but Frank this is a subject that requires a serious answer —
[Frank]	Why then upon my soul I never in my Life took the least Liberty with her — I beleive indeed she seem'd at one time to have taken a fancy to me — but she wasn't to my Taste so I gave her no encouragement —
[P.]	Why sure Frank — even if she had solicited you would not have consended[sic]
[Frank]	Why lookee Frank[sic] — I hope I shall never deliberately do a dishonourable — but if I [sic] a pretty woman were to fling her self in my way — and that pretty woman married — to a man twice old enough to be her Father — I swear I can't answer for myself —

to talk with you a little seriously —

Hey what's the matter now —

Why it seems something in your very conduct has alarm'd his jealousy — but I hope you are too much a man of honor ever to have given any cause for such a suspicion —

this ... will equal this in ridiculous envy, so the old Baronet begins to find his young wife want a better task than he thought —

Nay look Frank there is a subject that requires a serious answer —

Why then upon my soul I never in my life took the least liberty with her — I believe indeed she seem'd at one time to have taken a fancy to me — but she never was to my taste so I gave her no encouragement —

Why sure Frank — even if she had solicited you would not have consented

Why look Frances — I hope I shall never deliberately do a dishonorable — but if a pretty woman was to fling herself in my way — a that pretty woman married to a man twice old enough to be they father — I ... I can't answer for myself —

[P.]	But tell me seriously there never has anything pass'd —
[Frank]	Nay if I must be serious — I never upon my honor have had the smallest familiarity pass'd between us and what's more I give you my word I never had any such intention —
[P.]	Well — well this will be a great satisfaction to Sr Peter —
[Frank]	But upon my word Frank [sic] — you surprise me extremely — in mentioning — *me* as the object of for upon my word I always took *you* to be Lady Teazle's Favourite —
[P.]	Fie — fie — Frank —
[Frank]	Nay I swear I have seen her give you some very significant glances —
[P.]	Hush — sdeath ~~this~~ He'll out with something that may alarm Sr Peter — your raillery is ill timed — it is a sorry subject for mirth —
[Frank]	Nay upon my word I'm serious — if I'm not mistaken I have seen her call her[e] at your Lodgings —
[P.]	Indeed I beleive I had better call out Sr Peter
[Frank]	Nay — don't you remember one day — When we were at [?] Sr Peter's house —
[P.]	now as you have cleared yourself — entirely

But tell me seriously there never has anything pass'd —

Nay if I must be serious — I swear upon my honour have
had the smallest formality pass'd between us what
more I give you my word I never had any such intention —

Well — well this will bee a great satisfaction to
Sr Peter —

But upon my word Frank — you surprise me
extremely — in mentioning — me as the object of
for upon my word I always took you to
be Lady Teazle's favourite —

Mine — Miss — Frank.

Nay I swear I have seen her give you
some very significant glances —

Hush — I shall the he'll out with something
that may alarm Sr Peter — your will
will be the tinsel — it is a worthy subject
for mirth —

Nay upon my soul I'm serious — if indeed
hereditary I have seen her call her of
your lodgings —

Indeed I believe I had better call out Sr
Peter —

Nay — don't you remember one day —
— Oh no — and Sr Peter to bear —
— now at you have cleared yourself — what

— Sir Peter — appear —

[Frank]   Sir Peter — what the Devil Sir Peter there
                 hallo — Sr Peter —! Sr Peter come forth —

                          Enter Sr Peter

                 Hah! old jealousy — whose Plot was this?

[Sir P.]   Come give me your Hand Frank — I own
                 twas mine — I was taxing you to your Brother
                 and He was so positive of your Innocense —
                 that I made him consent to obtain Proof of it —
                 but what I've heard — has given me
                 great satisfaction —

[Frank]   Egad then it was well you heard no more
                 wasn't it ~~Frank~~ Tom —

[Sir P.]   but you mustn't take — it ill — of Tom — tho' you
                 would have retorted — on him —

[Frank]   Aye aye that was a Joke hey Tom —

[Sir P.]   Come — come — I knew Tom was a man
                 of too much Honour —

[Frank]   Yes yes I don't pretend to be so strict as Joseph —
                 here — but in this Point you might as
                 well suspect him as me //Mightn't he Frank//

                          Enter Serv — whispers —

Y Pl.   Sir Peter excuse me one moment —

[Frank]   No[w] I want to have a word or two with Sr Peter

                 //calls him Guardian //

Sir Peter — offer —

Sir Peter — returned the Domestic Police &c
vol 6 — Sir Peter — : Sir Peter comfortable —

— Enter Sir Peter

Hah! old jealousy — what Plot was this?
come give me your hand Frank — your
tutor's mine — I was taking you to your Master
& he was so positive of your Innocence
that I made them consent to give proof of it —
but what I've heard — has given me
general satisfaction —

Egad they it was well you heard no more
wan't it Frank Tom —

but you mustn't take it ill of Tom — tho' you
would have retorted on him —

Aye aye that was a Joke by Tom —

come — come — I knew Tom was a man
of too much honour —

Yes yes I don't pretend to be so strict as Joseph
here — but to in this Point you might as
well suspect him as me — might you Frank —
— say Frank —

— Enter Servt — whispers —

Sir Peter excuse me one moment
as I want to have a word or two with Sir Peter

Well — Sir — you must for the future lay aside your
suspicions — don't have an ill opinion because
He is now and then given a little to wenching — now
Here's sobersides my Brother — I suppose He
lives as chastely — as [a] cardinal — yet egad I don't
know that He is the Honester Fellow for't —

[Sir P.]   Ha! ha! come come — Joe is no woman hater —
neither — tho' he would not give into the fashionable
spirit of Intrigues —

[Frank]   O hang him — He'd sooner spend I don't
beleive he ever had an amour with
any creature above — a Housemaid — [illegible]
so apprehensive — of his good Name that
I suppose — [he would as soon] have a Priest in his Lodging
as a Pretty Girl.

//nothing is so noble as a man of Sentiment//

[Sir P.]   Ha! ha! that's good ifaith — but don't you
abuse him or perhaps He may hear of it
again —

[Frank]   would you tell him

[Sir P.]   No but — hearkee — here a little more
this way — the sly fellow had a Wench
with him when I called —

[Frank]   The Devil — was she Handsome —

[Sir P.]   Hush! the best of the Joke is she's in the
Room now — there — there — //Egad I have good mind to tell him//

[Frank]   Zounds lets have a Peep — at here [sic] —

Well – Sir – you must for the future lay aside your
suspicions – a don't have an ill opinion because
he is now & then given a little to wenching – now
sure's sobersides my Brother – I suppose the
lives as chastely – as covenial – yet egad I don't
know that he is the slowest fellow you! –

Harkee! come come – Joe is no woman hater –
neither – – tho' he would not give into the fashionable
spirit of Intrigues – –

I grant you him – he'll sooner spend I don't
believe he ever had – an amour with
any mistress above – a housemaid – he
so apprehensive – of his good Name that
I suppose – have a Priest in his lodging
as a pretty girl –

place me! nothing is so noble as a man of sentiment
that's good efaith – but clear your
face him or perhaps he may hear of it
again –
would you tell him

No but – hearke – have a little more
this way – the sly fellow had a woman
with him when I called –
the Devil – was she Handsome
steal! the best of the joke is she's
known ever – – there – there – Egad you to the Priar
I and let him have a peep – at home –

[Sir P.]	No no — not for — the world —
[Frank]	O by all means — we'll smoke the little Milliner —
[Sir P.]	Oh! — no hang it t'wont be fair — and Joe'll be angry — that I told you — you shan't upon my soul —
[Frank]	Egad but [I] will —
[Sir P.]	Idiot — fool! He's coming —

Enter — Surface
F. Knocks down the Screen — and discovers Lady
Teazle —

[Frank]	What the Devil! who have we here — Lady Teazle — by all thats wonderful —
[Sir P.]	— Lady Teazle — by all thats Damnable!
[Frank]	Why Sr Peter — hows this — this egad — she's the smartest French Millener that I ever saw — what dumb — Brother — Has Honour nothing to say for himself — well egad — but you all seem to have lost — your tongues — perhaps you'll argue better when I'm gone //I don't understand it — but I dare swear you'll make it very clear when I'm gone// so I'll e'en leave you to make it out among yourselves — Sr Peter what a Noble ~~thing~~ Being a man of sentiment is!

ex.

//A little Hyde and Seek
nothing but a little Blind man's Buff
among yourselves//

124

No no — not for the world —
I beg all means — well make the little
ruffian —

Oh! I — no hang if t'were't be fair — s. pet'r
be angry — that if I tell you — or you else! —
upon my soul — —

Egad but will —

I hear — fore! — He's coming —

exit — Surface

I — Noily down the Screen — 2 discover Lady Teazle

What the Devil! — who have we here — Lady
Teazle — by all that's wonderful —
— Lady Teazle — by all that's honorable!
Why Sir Peter — how's this — this equals —
she's the sweetest French milliner that
I ever saw — what! dumb — Brother —
Has Stewart nothing to say for himself —
well egad — I don't understand it — but I dare all seems to
because look — your temper — perhaps! —
it very dear when I'm gone — say you'll make
egad I'll expect better when I'm gone —
so I'll een leave you to make it
out among yourselves — Sir Pete
what a Noble Being a true of sentiment is!

125

YS	Sr Peter — I don't [wonder] at your being surprised — and I must confess that Appearances are against me — but — Sir — if you will give me leave I'll explain the whole in such manner —
[Sir P.]	If you please Sir
[YS]	Sir Lady Teazle Sir — knowing your Jealousy I say Sir — //Lady Teazle knowing your Jealousy// and my Friendship to the Family came here Sir expecting to find your Daughter — this is the whole truth —
[Sir P.]	It has a very probable air truly — your Lady - ship will I dare say vouch — for the Truth of it —
[Lady T.]	Not one syllable — of it Sir — Sr Peter —
[Sir P.]	How — the evidence — Differ —
[Lady T.]	There's not one word of truth in what that Gentleman — has told you —
[Sir P.]	I beleive it upon my soul Ma'am —
[YS]	Sdeath ma'am will you betray me —
[Lady T.]	Good — Mr Hypocrite — by your leave — I will — speak — for myself —
[Sir P.]	Aye let alone Sir — I dare swear she'll make out a better story without Prompting
[Lady T.]	Hear me — Sir Peter — I came hither today to

48   Sir Peter – I don't [wonder] at your being surprized – and I must
confess that Appearances are against me – but Sir –
if you will give me leave I'll explain the whole
in such manner –

If you please Sir –

Sir – Lady Teazle Sir – knowing your Jealousy
I say her – and my friendship to the Family
came here Sir expecting to find your Daughter –
this is the whole truth –

If has a very probable air truly – your Ladyship will I dare say vouch – for the Truth of
it –

Not one syllable – of it Sir – Sir Peter –

How – the evidence – Differ –

There's not one word of truth in what that Gentleman
has told you –

I believe it upon my soul Ma'am –

'Sdeath ma'am will you betray me –

Good – Mr. Hypocrite – by your leave –
I will – speak – for myself –

Aye let alone Sir – I dare swear you
make out a better story without Nonsense
–

Hear me – Sir Peter – I came hither to day

seek no Daughter nor to ask any Advince [sic] —
but — seduced — by that smooth tong'd Gentleman —
I forgot my Duty — and Integrity — and came
here to give him an opportunity to make
love to me —

[Sir P.]   Come now I beleive the Truth is coming —
aye aye this is brave [?] —

[YS]   The Womans mad —

[Lady T.]   No — Sir — I have recover'd my senses —
your — own Arts have given me an
opportunity of beholding you in so des-
picable a Light that I know not which
I disprize most myself or you —
Sr Peter — I do not deserve you to credit me
but — But the Tenderness you have shewn —
which I am sure you did not know I was
a witness to — have penetrated me to the
Heart and had I left this place without the
shame of this Discovery you should have
found it by my actions — as for that
Hypocrite who would have debauchd the
wife of his Friend while he was making
honourable proposals for the Daugh[t]er —

128

seek a vain daughter me to use my influence —
but — seduced — by that smooth tong'd Gentleman.
I forgot my Pity — & Integrity — and came
here to give them an opportunity to make
love to me —

Came now — I believe the Butler is coming —
and say there is here —

The Woman & men —

No — Sir — I have recover'd my senses —
your — own Arts have given me an —
opportunity of beholding you in so des=
=picable a light that I know not which
I despise most myself or you —

P. Pete. I do not desire you to credit me
but — But the Tenderness you have shewn —
which I am sure you did not know I was
a witness to — have penetrated me to the
heart & had I left this place without the
shame of this Discovery you then had been
found it by my actions — as for that
thy favorite who would have debauch'd the
wife of his friend while he was working
knavishly preposterous for the Daughter —

	He is [sic] shewn — himself in such a Light that

He is [sic] shewn — himself in such a Light that
I know not which must [sic] to despize myself //equally// for having
been delude[d] by such a wretch or his Baseness in
having attempted it —

[YS]   Sr Peter — notwithstanding these appearances
Heaven knows —

[Sir P.] That you are a Villain —
and mark me sir — I'm not so old — but
that I can hold a sword — I have given
you your Name — and if you are not [a] Coward —
~~you~~ I shall hear of it —

ex.

Act. 5th

we all agree that Sr Peter is mortally wounded.
Sr the Ball struck against his his Hat — grazed
out of the window //a Bronze Figure on the Chimney// and what's very
    remarkable — wounded the Post
man who had just knock'd at the Door with a
Letter from his Brother in Northamptonshire —
I have heard it from a Person who walk'd bye at the Time — He has
never been home yet — Here He comes let him be
be put to bed directly.
⟨Sr P. drives them out — then the old Steward.
Sr. Nol. reconciles them — Lad. T. and I'll live in the country
half the year.⟩

He is shewn himself in such a light that
I know not which most to despise myself for having
been deluded by such a wretch or the baseness in
having attempted it —

Sr Peter — notwithstanding these appearances
However —

That you are a Villain — —

A meaner one — I'm not so old — but
that I can hold a Sword — I have given
you your Name — if you are not coward
you shall hear of it —   .x.
                           Act 5th

we all agree that Sr Peter is mortally wounded
— S! the Ball struck against his Hat ...
out of a Bronze figure in the Passage which is very remarkable ..
the ... & wounded the Post.
man who has just knock'd at the Door with a
letter from his Brother in Northampton shire —
I have heard it from a Man who walk'd by at the Time .. He has
never been home yet — — When he comes let him be
be put to bed directly . .

——————— Sr P. Louis then out — then the old Steward . — — — —

Sr Nol recancles them — Lad. T.   & I'll live in the country
half the year.

⟨Act 1st S. 1st — Sr Peter and Stewart [sic] and Daughter — 2d Sr P. and Lady — maid and
    Steward — then young Plyable
Act 2 — Sr P. and Lady — with — young Harrier — Sr P. and Sr Rowland — and old
    Jeremy — Sr P. and Daughter. Y.P. and Y R. —
Act 3 — Sr R. Sr P and O.J. 3d Y.P. and Comp. with O R. and Y.R. and Maria — with Y̶P̶H.
    O R. and Young Harrier to borrow
Act 4. Y P. and Maria to borrow his money — gets away what he had rais'd from his uncle —
                Y P. old Jer. and Tradesmen — P. and Lady T. etc. —
                lay hold of the jew who was to lend him money.
                who discovers that He had some of the annuities
                of his own Brother —
        I'll ask 8 per cent
    how much then
    as you find he wants it — if you find him in great Distress —
    and want very — bad — you must ask double —
    would his Brother be his security
    I have his Name to the Bond
                                        — He is the Lender —
    But mustn't I alter my Dress — i[s]n't rather — too
    smart for a money Lender —
                O Lord — no Sir the thriving — you
    will not be at all out of character if you go in
    your own carriage —
                the great Point is to be exorbitant enough —
                you know I borrow it of a Friend —
                your Friend unreasonable — what a d-d rogue your
                Friend must be — a son of a jew — not you your
                                        Friend that lends the money
                I'll ask 8 per cent — fifty
                                        and Lease [?] with fifty
    Come Sir — Here's success to usury — fill the Gentleman [a] Bumper —
    — Nay if you talk of conscience — you're not the man I took you
    for — Here's little cent for cent — our Friend was kill'd in a Duel — He never gave me
    notice to ensure his Life — annuity on a Lady —
    — He'll be so long Introducing —
    come no ceremony — I'm an extravagant young [Fellow] that want —
    money to borrow — you I take to be a usurious — old Fellow that have
    got money to lend — I am Bloc[k]head enough to be willing
    to give fifty per Cent — and you I presume are Rogue enough
    to take 100 — if you could get it — Now Sir — I dare say
    we are acquainted at once — ⟩

Act 1st. 1st. sc: Sr Peter & Stewart — 2. Sr P. & Lady's-maid & Stewart — then young Plyable —
Act 2 - Sr P. & Lady — 9. young Harrier — Sr P. & Sr Rowland — & old Jeremy — Sr R. daughter. Y Sr P. —
Act 3: Sr R. Sr P. & 9. 3. Y P. & comp. 9s OR. 2 9. R. — & Maria — Sr 4th. OR. & young Harrier —
Act 4. Y P. & maria — to borrow the money — got away what he had rais'd from his uncle — to Graham

2 Daughter

— Y P. old Jer. & Tradesmen — P & Lady J. & c — —

lay hold of 9 Jew who was to lend him money.
who discovers that He had some of the annuities
of his own Brother —

now much ask 8 per cent

as you find he wants it — if you find him in great Distress
& want very — bad — you want it be double —
would his Brother be his security

I have his Name to the Bond —

— He is the lender —

But must it I alter my dress — it's rather too
smart for a money lender —

I lend — no to the thriving — you
will not be at all out of character if you go in
your own carriage —

the great Point is to be exorbitant enough
you know I borrow it of a Friend
your friend persevere... — in fact a I — & rogue you
Friend may go — a son of a gun & not you your
I'll ask I per at — fifty Friend that lend the mon

Come Sir — Here's success to Usury fill the gentle Bump
2 Peace with
— Nay if you talk of conscience — you've not the man I took you
for — Here's little cent per cent over disigned it was still in a dwel
notice to entering his life — / annuity on a Lady —
& He'll be so long introducing —
come no ceremony — I'm an extravagant young that want
money — you I take to be a jemison — old fellow that have
got money to lend — I am Blockhead enough to be willing
to give fifty per cent — & you I presume one forever enough
to take 100. if you could get it — now Sir — I dare say
acquainted at once

⟨Roundhead [?] in Barber [?] Lesson

if he was to lose a Hair whenever he tells a lie
He'd be bald in four and twenty Hours —

    going to Julia they are to leave their Wives and their consciences at Home

Servants used to have only the cast vices of their masters — but now they have
him [sic] like their Birth Day Cloath with the Gloss on them

       why should you think this Feat so improbable
     because it is so criminal

       humble from Praise and timorous thro' success

       to dress in Bags and Bouquet —

A wife with her Gallant entrusted in a mask — to her own
Husband — who treacherously attempts her — Gallant comes in upbraids
him with this breach of confidence — discovery — the marriage a
conceal'd one — the men intimate Friends — Gallant — tired sends
his Friend in his Place — who finds his own Wife — or he discovering
the appointment — goes treacherously — and pretend to be Gallant —

He let himself be cheated by Strangers tho' I was always at hand
and had known him from a Child — and if his Flatterers call
him Shylock —

     The Dogs send in such extravagant Bills and
     paying them is only encouraging them — ⟩

if he was to lose a Hair whenever Roundow in Backo Lesson —
He'd be bald in four & twenty Hours — "

going to Subathey are to leave their Wives & their consciences at Home.

mankind used to have only the cast view of their master — but now they wear
him like their Birth Day Cloath with the gloss on them

why should you think this Fact so improbable
because it is so criminal.

humble from Praise & timorous their success

of to dress in Bays & Bouquet —

A wife with her gallant entrusted in a mask — to her own
Husband — who treacherously attempts her — Gallant comes in upbraids
him — with this breach of confidence — discovery — the marriage a
conceal'd one — the men intimate Friends — Gallant tired sends
his Friend in his Place — who finds his own Wife — or he discovering
the appointment — goes treacherously & pretend to be Gallant —

He let himself be cheated by Strangers tho' 'twas always at hand
& had known him from a Child — his Flatterers call
him Shylock —

The Dog used in such exlooveragess Bills and
norrig letter is over exercised them —

⟨Crabtree to wear a Muff — ⟩

unable to wear a Muff –

Act 4th

Scene 1st

Surface's Lodgings

Surface and Servant

Surf.   — 'Sdeath you Blockhead you should have
said I was gone out of Town, or sick or
anything sooner than have let the Fellow stay
to teaze me now — you know I expect
Lady Teazle to call this morning. —

Serv.   — Upon my word, Sir, He was so importunate
I knew not what to do — He insisted on
staying 'till you came in and said He was
sure you would be glad to see him.

Surf.   — Glad to see him indeed — Why the Fellow
comes a begging — A Relation of my Mothers
as He pretents [sic] — ~~says his Name~~ says his
Name is Stanley doesn't He —

Serv.   Yes Sir — but He doesn't carry himself as
if He came to ask the Favours —

Surf.   Yes — yes I know his Errand — He has plagued
me with Letters. — well I must see
him —

ex. Serv.

Act 4.th

Scene 1.st

<u>Surface's</u> Lodgings

<u>Surface</u>. & Servant.

Surf. – 'Sdeath you Blockhead you should have
said I was gone out of the Town or sick or
anything sooner than have let the Fellow stay
to tearze me now – you know I expect
Lady Teazle to call this morning. –

Serv. – Upon my word Sir, He was so importunate
I knew not what to do – He insisted on
staying till you come in & said He was
sure you would be glad to see him.

Surf – Glad to see him indeed – Why the Fellow
comes a begging – A Relation of my Mother's
as He pretents – says his Name & says his
Name is Stanley does'nt He –

Serv. – Yes Sir. but He does'nt carry himself as
if he came to ask the Favour. –

Surf. – Yes – yes I know his Errand – He has plagued
me with Letters . – well I must see
him –

Ex. Serv.

⟨I am afraid I have brought you too abruptly — I don't
[know] how I shall break you to him — for his Nerves
are so weak — the sight of a poor Relation may
be too much for him⟩

I am afraid I have brought you too abrubtly – I don't
know I shall break you to him – for his Nerves
are so weak – the sight of a poor Relation may
be too much for him

This is one bad Effect of a good Character!
it invites applications from the unfortunate
and it requires no small Degree of Address
to gain the Reputation of Benevolence without
the expence of it — I must leave Directions
to be interrupted as soon as possible

ex.
Enter Serv. and Sr Oliver

Serv.   My Master — Sir was here this Instant —
                  He will speak to you in a moment — tho'
                  He was very angry with me for suffering
                  you to see him.

Sr Ol.   Impossible Fellow if you told him [who] I was —

Serv.   O Lud, Sir, Thence rose his Anger — Sir my
                  my master has wonderful weake nerves — He
                  swounds at the sight of a Poor Relation.

Sr Ol.   He is known to be a man of a most bene-
                  volent way of Thinking —

Serv.   True Sir — I will venture to say He has
                  as much speculative Benevolence as any
                  private Gentleman in the Kingdom —

Sir Ol.   Tis a heavenly Virtue.

Serv.   Yes Sir and what makes it more esti-
                  mable in him is his great self denial in
                  the exercise of it — for tho' you may know

this is one bad Effect of a good Character! it invites applications from the unfortunate and it requires no small Degree of Address to gain the Reputation of Benevolence without the expence of it – – I must leave Directions to be interrupted as soon as possible (ex.)

Enter Serv. & Sir Oliver

Serv. My Master – Sir was here this Instant – He will speak to you in a moment – tho' He was very angry with me for suffering you to see him –

Sir Ol. Impossible Fellow if you told him I was –

Serv. O Lud, Sir, There rose his Anger – Sir my my master has wonderful weake nerves – He sobbedle at the sight of a Poor Relation.

Sir Ol. He is known to be a man of a most bene= =volent way of Thinking –

Serv. True Sir – I will venture to say He has as much speculative Benevolence as any private Gentleman in the Kingdom –

Sir Ol. Tis a heavenly Virtue –

Serv. Yes Sir, and what makes it more esti= =mable in him is his great self-denial in the exercise of it – for tho' you may know

⟨His common Conversation on the subject would
serve to open ~~the~~ an Hospital Chappel⟩

leave the Room

His common conversation on the subject would tend to open the an Hospital Chappel

leave the Room

by his conversation that his Bosom is
full of it — yet has his Philosophy denies him
so sensual as to indulge himself in the exercise of it — they
say Chartity [sic] begins at home — but my Masters
is of that domestic //the only domestic Virtue He has for it not only
　　　begins at home// sort that never stirs
abroad at all — it is a maxim with him
that most of the misfortunes in this World
are Judgements and that it is impious for
another to prevent their operation —
//and so far from being asham'd of poor Relations//

Surf.　　　　　　Sir — I am informed you wish'd to speak with
　　　　　　　　me —

Sr Ol.　　　　　　You Sir I presume are Mr Surface —

Surf.　　　　　　I am — Sir — have you any particular Business — ?

Sr Ol.　　　　　　My Name Sir — is Stanley — I have taken the Liberty [of]
　　　　　　　　~~writing~~ informing you by Letter of my situation — and
　　　　　　　　have now attended you for that Releif which I doubt
　　　　　　　　not your generousity will yeild to the Distresses of
　　　　　　　　a Relation. —

Surf.　　　　　　Sir the Man who cannot feel for the Distresses
　　　　　　　　of a Fellow Creature — deserves never to know the
　　　　　　　　blessings of Prosperity — you were nearly related to
　　　　　　　　to my Mother — ?

[Sr Ol.]　　　　　I was Sir, nearer than perhaps her wealthy kindred would
　　　　　　　　chuse to own — else I had not presumed to ~~own~~
　　　　　　　　trouble you —

[Surf.]　　　　　O Sir do not name that — He that is [in] Distress tho'

146

by his conversation that his Bosom is full of it — yet has his Philosophy denies him
so natural as to indulge himself in the exercise of it. — they say Charity begins at home, but my Master is of that domestic the only domestic Virtue fool that never stirs abroad at all. — it is a maxim with him that most of the misfortunes in this World are Judgements and that it is impious for another to prevent their operation —

and so far from being ashamed of poor Relations

Surf. Sir — I am informed you wish'd to speak with me —

1st Oc. You Sir I presume are Mr. Surface —

Surf. I am — Sir — have you any particular Business — ?

1st Oc. My Name Sir — is Stanley — I have taken the Liberty writing informing you by Letter of my Situation — and have now attended you for that Relief which I doubt not your generosity will yeild to the Distresses of a Relation. —

Surf. Sir the Man who cannot feel for the Distresses of a Fellow creature — deserves never to know the Blessings of Prosperity — you were nearly related to to my mother — ?

I was Sir, nearer than perhaps her wealthy kindred would chuse to own — else I had not presumed to trouble you —

O Sir do not name that — He that is Distress the

⟨if my Poverty makes you blush to own me for
you[r] Relation — releive if not from Pity from Pride. — ⟩

if my Poverty makes you blush to own me for
you Relation _ relieve if not from Pity from Pride. _

	a Stranger has a right to claim kinddred with the wealthy — and I wish from my Heart I was of the Latter Class and had it [in] my Power to releive you —
Sr Ol.	— Sure Sir you do not pretend that you have not the Ability to releive me if you please —
Surf.	I assure — you Sir — there is very little in my Power.
[Sr Ol.]	If your Unkle Sr Oliver were here I should not [want] a Friend —
Surf.	I am sure I wish He was with all my heart — I would be your advocate I assure you —
Sr Ol.	I should not need it Sir — but I imagined He ~~But~~ had enabled you to pay the Tribute which Charity looses by his Absence —
Surf.	Alas — Sir — you are strang[e]ly misinformed — Sr Oliver is very good but the allowance he has transmitted has never been liberal tho' People I know have thought otherwise — ~~an~~
[Sr Ol.]	Ungrateful Fellow!
[Surf.]	And then Sir //Mr Stanley// I doubt you have heard of my extravagant Brother — 'tis not know[n] what straights I have put myself to — to serve him — in short Sir I have envolved myself so that I have

150

a stranger has a right to claim kindred with
the wealthy — and I wish from my heart
I were of the latter Class & had it my power
to relieve you. —

S. Ol. — Sure Sir you do not pretend that you have
not the Ability to relieve me if you please. —

Sir. I assure — you Sir — there is very little in
my Power.
If your Humble S:r Oliver were here I should
not a friend —

Sub. I am sure I wish He was with all my heart — I
would be your advocate I assure you —
I should not need it Sir — but I imagined He
had enabled you to pay the Tribute which
Charity losses by his Absence —

Surf. Alas — Sir — you are strongly misinformed — S:r
Oliver is very good but the allowance he has transmitted
has never been [what?] tho' People I know have
thought otherwise — an
Ungrateful Fellow!
And then Sir, [more plainly] I doubt you have heard of my
Extravagant Brother — 'tis not know what straights
I have put myself to — to serve him — in short
Sir I have involved myself so that [these]

	it not now in my Power to gratify my wishes in rel[e]iving you —
[Sr Ol.]	You have lent Frank money —
[Surf.]	O Frequently! —
[Sr Ol.]	Hum — what a lying Hypocrite it is —
[Surf.]	But Sir if hereafter it should be in my Power you shall certainly hear from me. —
[Sr Ol.]	What, Sir, can you do nothing Now —
[Surf.]	Truly Sir — it is not in my Power — and my Pain in refusin[g] is equal to yours — Sir — the man who begs — feels not such Distress as He who wishes and has it not in his Power to releive —
Sr Ol.	A small matter even.
Surf.	There Sir — for the Present — I wish my ability was greater —
Sr Ol.	Half a guinea — Benevolent Sir — ! I am your Relation oppress'd as you know with un- wonted misfortune a wif[e] and infant family the Partners of my Distress — you give half a guinea to my Necessities the Price of an opera [ticket] — there Sir — I scorn your Pitiful Bounty as yourself — your Pretended Benevolence and affected charity can[not] impose on me and perhaps you may shortly repent that your narrow soul has betray'd you — Charles — you'r my Heir —

exit —

Enter Serv —

[Surf.]	An impudent Fellow — a very Sturdy Beggar. So Sir your folly has cost me a Sum

it not more in my Power to gratify my wishes
in relieving you —

You have lent Frank money —

O Imequrafer, —

them — what a lying Hypocrite it is —

But Sir if hereafter it should be in my Power
you shall certainly hear from me — —

What Sir, can you do nothing Now —

Truly Sir — it is not in my Power — and my Pain
in refusing is equal to yours — Sir the man who begs
feels not such Distress as He who wishes & has it not in
his Power to relieve —

P.R. A small matter even.

Surf. There Sir — for the Present. I wish my ability
was greater — —

P.R. Half a guinea — Benevolent Sir —! I am your
Relation offpring as you know with an-
wanted misfortune a wife & infant family
the Partner of my Distress who you give half
a guinea to my Neceffity — there Sir — I scorn
your pitiful Bounty u yourself — your husband
Benefactors & affected charity can impose on
me & perhaps you may thereby repent that
your reason will have betray'd y ours —
                    Charles — your my heir —   Exit.
Enter Love —

An impudent Fellow — a very Sturdy Beggar.
to Sir your folly has cost me a sum

[Serv.]   — He is gone Sir muttering strange Threats —

[Surf.]   Well let him Starve — This will serve for the Opera.

– He is gone his muttering storms [illegible] –
Will let him Storm – This will serve for the Opera.

Surf.	— Hark — This must be Lady Teazle see whether it is or not before you go down —

(throws up the Sash

Serv.	Yes Sir — 'tis she my Lady and alone — she generally leaves [her] carriage at the Milleners —

Surf.	~~But~~ stay — ~~Frank~~ draw that Screen before the Window — my opposite Neighbours are the most inquisitive Crew!

(ex. Serv.

~~What~~ a very difficult Part I have to play here —
I must by no means shrink from the Pursuit of
Maria — yet have the spright[l]y Attractions of this little
Rustic stole into my Heart so that I am led to
risk my Interest with Sr Peter — and sacrifice my
Policy to my Passion —

— Enter Lady Teazle —

Lad.	Alone — have you been very impatient? — come now don't pretend to look grave — I vow I couldn't come before —

Surf.	O Madam — Punctuality is a species of Constancy ~~not~~ a virtue which I never expect to find in a woman.

[Lady T.]	Upon my word you must pity me do you know that Sr Peter is grown so jealous of me that He watches all my Actions —

[Surf]	Then dear it becomes a Point of Honour to deceive him —

'Surf — # Hark — this must be Lady Teazle see
whether it is or not before you go down —

- Servt — .... [throws up the door]

Yes — tis she — my Lady's alone — she generally leaves carriage
at the Milliners —

Surf — But stay — Frank .... draw thof Screen
before the Window — my opposite Neighbours are
the most inquisitive Crew !

[Ex. Servt.

Part
What a very difficult ^ I have to play here —
I must by no means shrink from the Pursuit of
Maria — yet have the sprightly Attractions of this little
Rustic stole into my Heart so that I am led to
risk my Interest with Sir Peter — & sacrifice my
Policy to my Passion —

— Enter Lady Teazle —

Lad. Alone — have you been very impatient? — come
now don't pretend to look grave — I vow I
wouldn't come before — ######

Surf — O Madam — Punctuality is a species of Constancy
and a virtue which I never expect to find in
a woman.
Upon my word you wrong me do you
know that Sir Peter is grown so jealous
of me that He watches all my Actions — — — —
Then dear it becomes a Point of Honour to decive
him —

⟨if I'm not to do as I like you know what does He
think I married him for — ~~He is as~~ I might as well
have lived with my Father in the country — to thrown [?]

don't make a Fool of your Husband
and let him suspect you without cause

when a Husband suspects his wife without
Reason She should compliment his Discernment by giving him
cause —

There is no way of curing him of his
Jealousy but by giving him reason for it.⟩

if I'm not to do as I like, you know what does he think I married him for — Heavens I might as well have lived with my Father in the country -- to thrown --

don't make a Fool of your Husband
& let him suspect you without cause
when a Husband suspects his wife without
Reason she should confirm his discernment by giving him
cause -

There is no way of curing him of his
jealousy but by giving him reason for it -

if He reposed confidence in you — you owe it to yourself —
to be faithful to him — but when a Husband — trys his —
wit against his wife — the compact is broke and she
owes it to the honor of her sex to outwit him —

[Lady T.]   Indeed it is cruelly provoking now when I know the
integrity of my own heart — and that I have never wrong'd
him — to have him enternally [sic] suspicious, teazing, and dissatisfied
— worse he could not be if I had served him as he merits —

[Surf.]   'tis very cruell indeed —

[Lady T.]   And then to have all the malicious Things in the
world reported of one — and all the scandalous
Tales — with[out] any Foundation too that's what vexes
me —

[Surf.]   Aye Madam — to be sure — that is the provoking
Circumstance — without Foundation — //yes yes theres the// when a
    scan-
dalous Tale is reported [sic] — of one there is no Comfort
like — the consciousness of [having] deserved it — that is
my — sentiment Madam —

[Lady T.]   — To be sure and a very proper Sentiment too —

            //make love thro the understanding — //

if He reposed confidence in you – you owe it to yourself –
to be faithful to him – but when a Husband – trusts his –
wife – the compact is broken and the –
owes it to the honor of her sex to outwit him –
Indeed it is cruelly provoking now when I know the
integrity of my own heart – & that I have never wrong'd
him – to have him externally suspicious, teazing, & dissatisfied
– & worse he could not be if I had served him as the world –
'tis very cruel indeed, –

And then to have all the malicious things in the
world reported of one – and all the scandalous
Tales – with any foundation too that what vexes
me –

Ay Madam – to be sure that is the provoking
Circumstance – without foundation – when a scan-
-dalous Tale is reported – if one there is no comfort
like – the consciousness of deserved it – that is
my – sentiment Madam –

–: To be sure of a very proper Sentiment too –

make love thro' the understanding –

⟨Pistols charge to go to [illegible]
The Servant denies his being at home — to conceal —
    Him — the Doctor —
        Snake confess forging Letter
        [illegible] — Lady Sneerwell — and Surf — goes into Closet
        our Thanks are due to Rowley
    Rowley to end —
    Do tell us the circumstances you may depend on't
    they shall go no further —
    as to reforming — I rather think I shall not —
        Surf — goes off with a Sentiment
    Let 'em marry — like oil and vinegar —
    Bromfield[?] [illegible] — and Hawkins Role
    Surf — I'm sure Sir — I could vindicate myself
    entirely —
    — and you two [sic] Sir —
    — Not I upon — my Soul Sir —
    Innocent
    guilty
    Sr O. Hypocrite — Shame —
    O Lud if He speaks so to Honesty — what will He
    say to me — //we began// we had given you over
    you are just come in time to save your life
    be tied
    you'll be greatly   Half the [illegible]
    tis a damd wicked world we live in
    you musn't mind
    People laughing   disapointing them — by paying 'em
    egad so is this is the
    most sudden recovery
    a world for the young Men
    and Sr Peter was never mistaken in his Life —
    discernment
    what you don't stand up for ~~the~~ Your
    honest ~~Joseph~~ Friend Joseph
    O Yes I do — they are very honest
    [two lines illegible]
    //his Impudence comes very near to a Virtue
    Snake was to swear that they were contracted
    if you will kill him
    cant you kill a man without a Doctor//⟩

162

The servant denies his being at home — to conceal —
Home — the Doctor —

make countess longing better
under. Lady Percivill — I dont — you into looked
our thanks are due to Rowley.

Rowley to end —

Do tell us the circumstances you may depend as
they shall go no too far —
as to reforming — I rather think I shall not —
such — goes off with a sentiment
Let 'em marry — like oil & vinegar —

Rosefield — a touching &c

Joseph — I am sure Sir — I could vindicate myself
entirely —
and you too Sir —
Not Inferior — very Sir — Sir —
I innocent
guilty —

1st O. Hypocrite — Knave —

O Lord if He speaks so to Honesty — what will the
_ say to me — we had given you over
you are just come in time to save
Half the cursing
die a damn'd wicked world an live in
+ disappointing them by paying em — egad to a that a the
a model for the young men
and Old Peter was never mistaken in his type
discounts
what you don't stand up for the young
honest Joseph
O yes I do

163

⟨Sk. for Sk.

A sort of Brokers in Scandal — who *transfer* lies without Fees — reputation like the Stocks —

mischief between Sr Peter

Tis — very convenient to our Plot that the Houses are so near —

does Sr [P] found out that He has got a young
wife —
No I am afraid she has discover'd that she has got
an old Husband

Lady Teazle has wit — and great virtue she and Charles —
Tie up the Knocker of her Tongue

Lady Sneerwell — to be with young Surface
angry — Charles's slight — tho' I offer'd to pay
his Debts — that Villian Snake —
put Charles's name as regularly into a Bond
as John Doe in a polity
among the Scandal/ — speculative Benevolence —
to have preserved five Houses etc.
A little starv'd Brat —
The Destinies in Tapestry —
I would say it [to] her Face — Sr Babble bore
Tis a left handed Cupid — for she squints like a fury —
if he was to lose a Hair whenever He tells a lie —

I must take leave of my Relations and not one [re]moves his Hat

Sr O. and R.   Like Birth Day Cloaths with the Gloss on —

Birth Day Cloaths — ⟩

A sort of Brokers in Scandal. who transfer lies without Fees. reputation like of Stocks.

mischief between t. Peter

Tis very convenient to our Plot that the Houses are so near.

since 1st found out that He begot a young

wife

No Jam afraid she has discover'd that she has got

an old Husband.

_____

+ Lady Teazle has wit - - & such virtue she & Charles.

Tie up the Knocker of her Tongue

_____

Lady Sneerwell - to be with young confess

angry - Charles's slight - tho' I offer'd to pay

his Debts. - that Villain Snake. -

put Charles his name as regularly into a Bond

as John Doe in a Lease.

among the Scandal of - Speculative Benevolence.

to have preserved two Houses & c -

A little stewn'd Brat. - — — —

The Destinies in Tapestry -

I would say it her Face - 1st Babble bore -

Tie a left handed Pupil - for she squints like a fury -

if he was to lose a Hair whenever he tells a lie -

I must take leave of my Relation & not one worse His.

Birth day Cloaths

Sho. 2 Ro. Line with the Gloss on - - -

Birth Day Cloaths -

*This book is set in 11 point Baskerville and is based
on the 1757 type of John Baskerville of Birmingham, England.
The paper is Mohawk Superfine Smooth White, which conforms to
the guidelines adopted by the Committee on Book Longevity of
the Council on Library Resources. The binding material is
Brillianta, a rayon cloth made by Van Heek-Scholco
Textielfabrieken, Holland. The composition and
printing are by Princeton University Press.
Designed by Bruce Campbell.*